Hope Jacobson
156-4001 Old Clayburn Rd
Abbotsford BC
V3G 1C5

Gwen to Virginia Moore
by. Kathy Smith
Dec '03.

# BY HIS STRIPES

*"Christ was treated as we deserve,*
*that we might be treated as He deserves.*
*He was condemned for our sins,*
*in which He had no share, that we might be*
*justified by His righteousness,*
*in which we had no share.*
*He suffered the death which was ours,*
*that we might receive the life*
*which was His.*
*'With His stripes we are healed.'"*
*—DA, 25*

## CLIFFORD GOLDSTEIN

**Pacific Press® Publishing Association**
Nampa, Idaho
Oshawa, Ontario, Canada

Edited by B. Russell Holt
Designed by Tim Larson
Cover art by Justinen Creative Group

Copyright © 1999 by
Pacific Press® Publishing Association
Printed in the United States of America
All Rights Reserved

Old Testament Bible quotations not otherwise credited are the author's
personal translation.
New Testament Bible quotations not otherwise credited are from the
King James Version.

Goldstein, Clifford
    By his stripes  /  Clifford Goldstein
        p.    cm.
    Includes bibliographical references.
    ISBN 0-8163-1699-6 (alk. paper)
    1. Bible. O.T. Isaiah—Criticism, interpretation, etc.  2. Christian
life—Adventist authors.  I. Title.
BS1515.2.G6   1999
224'.106—dc21                                             98-37463
                                                              CIP

99 00 01 02 03 • 5 4 3 2 1

# CONTENTS

*"Between us and heaven or hell
there is only life, which is the frailest
thing in the word."*
*—Pascal*

# Knocking on Heaven's Gate

*"To enjoy true happiness we must travel into a very far country, and even out of ourselves."*
*—Thomas Browne, c. 1680*[1]

Yvonne McCurdy-Hill had it right. Gail Maeder too. So did David Moore, John Craig, and Thomas Nichols. All were right to believe their leader, "Do," who warned that, because the planet was "about to be recycled,"[2] they had to get off.

The apostles Peter and Paul, in the wee hours of the preceding millennium, expressed similar sentiments. Paul explained how we leave:

> For the Lord himself shall descend from heaven with a shout, with the voice of the archangel, and with the trump of God: and the dead in Christ shall rise first: Then we which are alive *and* remain shall be caught up together with them in the clouds, *to meet the Lord in the air: and so shall we ever be with the Lord* (1 Thessalonians 4:16, 17, italics supplied).

Peter explained why we must: "But the day of the Lord will come as a thief in the night; in which the heavens shall pass away with a great noise, and the elements shall melt with fervent heat, the earth also and the works that are therein shall be burned up" (2 Peter 3:10).

The cyber-cultists, however—deciding not to wait for the Lord—tried to do it themselves. Unfortunately, phenobarbital, vodka, and asphyxiation, instead of lifting them above the earth, dumped them six feet under it. They might as well have tried drawing a four-sided triangle or counting to infinity on their fingers.

Yet no matter how weird their haircuts, androgyny, or theology, the misguided computer monks in Rancho Santa Fe were correct about one thing: time is short, our "containers" are decaying, and the earth will be recycled. No wonder they wanted out.

Centuries ago, Christian mystic Blaise Pascal wrote: "It is not to be doubted that the duration of this life is but a moment; that the state of death is eternal, whatever may be its nature; and thus all our actions and thoughts must take such different directions according to the state of that eternity."[3] With the logical precision of the great mathematician he was, Pascal argued that the inevitable shortness of this life, contrasted to the inevitable eternity that follows, makes preparing for what follows, whatever that may be, the only reasonable course. "We do not require great education of the mind," he wrote, "to understand there is no real and lasting satisfaction; that our pleasures are only vanity; that our evils are infinite; and lastly, that death, which threatens us every moment, must infallibly place us within a few years under the dreadful necessity of being forever either annihilated or unhappy."[4]

Thus, however macabre, there was a logic to the madness of the Heaven's Gate mass death, an almost syllogistic rationale to the cyber-cultists' suicide-in-stages. The world is, after all, decaying—and certainly (as anyone who's reached forty can attest) our bodies are too. So if one could circumvent the uncomfortable evanescence of our physical presence and elude the inevitable doom that looms in the future of us all, then the only rational thing would be—*to do it.*

Which is precisely what "Do" and Company did. They were not

alone. The Solar Temple faithful, who arranged themselves in a cross around a queen-sized bed before purposely being blown to bits, had the same problem: right logic, wrong premises. Instead of Hale-Bopp, though, the destination of the Solar Temple cult was the star Sirius, in the constellation Canis Major, nine light-years from Quebec, where "they will reign . . . forever, weightless and serene."[5]

Phenobarbital and bombs aside, one can understand the appeal in getting out of here, whether "weightless and serene" on Sirius or on the back of a UFO. In fact, the UFO craze is just another manifestation of humanity's desire to find meaning beyond what our short, pitiful, little spasm of cellular metabolism offers before a pipe breaks and we sputter into the nothingness from which we came. If we're stuck on earth, on our own, with obnoxious people like Timothy McVeigh and Leona Helmsly, and no one or nothing else is really out there—what can it all mean?

Yet the seeming meaninglessness of life is a fact most humans can't accept, which is why we are so susceptible to farfetched fantasies such as the New Age eschatology of former car-thief-turned-UFO-guru Marshall Herff Appelwhite, a k a "Do."

"UFOs," wrote Joel Achenbach of the *Washington Post*, "have gone new age. The UFO field has gradually been tugged away from the traditional phenomena of sightings, from the nuts and bolts of mysterious objects. Now the field is increasingly preoccupied with mystical, personal, subjective encounters with aliens, the abductions, the matings, the carrying of alien fetuses, the channeling of glib, pedantic, British-accented extraterrestrials from a tiny constellation known as the Pleiades."[6]

Recently, John Mack, a Harvard psychiatrist, published *Abduction: Human Encounters With Aliens*[7] (Charles Scribner's Sons), in which he claims that many earthly mortals have been abducted by UFOs.

What's fascinating about these documented claims is how often they resemble Near Death Experiences (NDEs), in which people who

have died come back to life and give fantastic descriptions of the
"other side," including the sensation of leaving their bodies and coming toward some sort of powerful light. And, just like those who "return from death," the alien abductees also testify to a new level of
spirituality following their otherworldly experience.

"I became more tolerant, more open-minded," said one woman,
in the *Atlantic Monthly*, after what she believed was an encounter
with a UFO. "I know now that there are many paths to the same God
and that God is the same no matter what you call Him."[8]

"Many abduction experiences are unequivocally spiritual," writes
Mack, "which usually involves some sort of powerful encounter with,
or immersion in, divine light. A number of abductees with whom I
have worked experience at certain points an opening in the source of
being in the cosmos, which they often call Home, and from which
they feel they have been brutally cut off in the course of becoming
embodied as a human being. They may weep ecstatically when during our sessions they experience an opening or return to Home. They
may rather resent having to remain on Earth in embodied form, even
as they realize that on Earth they have some sort of mission to assist
in bringing about a change in human consciousness."[9]

Sounds like Shirley McClaine meets *My Favorite Martian*.

And it's meant to. The enemy of souls is nothing if not in tune
with the times and trends; in fact, he establishes them, and in the
scientific, rationalistic, technologically advanced twentieth century,
UFOs will work better than ouija boards and seances to dupe a generation—raised on *Star Trek* and Pentiums—with a goofy sentimental-
ism that gives us an I'm-OK-You're-OK type of religion, a spiritual
Prozac that helps us cope with everything from co-dependency to
Attention Deficit Disorder.

Whether dangling from a tree in Eden or speaking through
Marshall Herff Applewhite, Satan has masterfully manipulated
mankind's innate needs, desires, and fears, for he understands them
so well. Because we were never meant to suffer the things that sin

has so universally wrought—pain, angst, fear, loneliness, emptiness, hopelessness, unhappiness, and death—there's something in our natures, something inherent in our genes, something (to borrow language from Austrian psychiatrist Carl Jung) perhaps almost archetypical in us that longs for relief from death, fear, loneliness, etc.—all the unnatural attributes that sin has made an integral part of the human condition. However it's expressed, manifested, or understood, what we are really seeking, from our DNA outward, is what we lost in Eden—an existence free from these pains.

Therefore, in innumerable guises, covers, and packages (yoga, Transcendental Meditation, Dianetics, papal indulgences, UFOs, whatever) Satan holds out false but beautiful promises of getting us back to what we once enjoyed in our garden home. Keenly aware of man's innermost desire, the devil leads us on endless paths of spirituality just as long as it's not the straight narrow one that, Jesus said, "leadeth unto life" (Matthew 7:14). And if Satan could dupe unfallen, perfect Eve (DNA fresh from the Creator's fingers), what kind of deceptions can he now pawn off on fallen, sin-laden souls thousands of years from the tree of life?

Just about any, as the Heaven's Gate fiasco has shown.

"People are hungry for transcendence," wrote John Whitehead. "They want to feel and know God. Seeking spirituality, they investigate the occult, angels, UFOs and extraterrestrial beings."[10]

All this desperate grappling for answers, for meaning, for transcendence—even to the point where seekers would take the short step from swallowing Applewhite's theology to swallowing his applesauce—are manifestations of man's endless quest for the one thing lost in Eden, and that is, happiness.

"God created the earth," Ellen White wrote, "to be the abode of holy, happy beings."[11]

And those happy, holy beings were to be humans. A loving God is going to create only happy people, as our first parents were in the beginning. Happiness was as much a part of our original being as were two eyes and a mouth. After the fall, although we took eyes and mouths from Eden, happiness (for the most part) was left behind. And since then, everyone, one way or another, by one means or another, has been trying to get it back, even if we're so far from it we don't know how to get it, how to keep it, or even what it really is.

"It is a misfortune," wrote Immanuel Kant, "that the concept of happiness is so indefinite that, although each person wishes to attain it, he can never definitely and self-consciously state what it is he really wishes and wills."[12]

The famous jurist Blackstone, in his *Commentaries on the Laws of England*, saw man's desire for happiness as a God-given natural law. "[T]hat man should pursue his own happiness," he wrote, "is the foundation of what we call ethics or natural law. For the several articles into which it is branched in our systems, amount to no more than demonstrating that this or that action tends to man's happiness, and therefore justly concluding that the performance of it is a part of the law of nature; or, on the other hand, that this or that action is destructive of man's real happiness, and therefore that the law of nature forbids it."[13]

In *Nicomachean Ethics*, Aristotle argued that the *summum bonum*, the supreme good of life, was happiness—and that the ultimate end of all that man does, the one thing that is complete in itself, and attained for no other purpose other than itself, is happiness.

"That which is always choosable," he wrote, "for its own sake and never because of something else, we call final without any qualification. Well, happiness more than anything else is thought to be just such an end, because we always choose it for itself, and never for any other reasons. . . . Happiness, then, is found to be something perfect and self-sufficient, being the end to which all our actions are directed."[14]

Mortimer Adler, echoing Aristotle, wrote that whatever we want—

wealth, power, freedom, knowledge—we want for the sake of something else. "But," explained Adler, "it is impossible to complete the sentence beginning with the words, 'We want to be happy or want happiness *because.* . . .' "[15]

Adler and Aristotle have a point. Why do people do what they do, except with the hope, however faint or ambiguous, of "happiness"? Who purposely does what will make himself unhappy? And even those who, in the short run, might do unpleasant things, do so hoping that, in the long run, they will achieve happiness.

Did the Heaven's Gate people kill themselves for any reason other than the hope of happiness in Hale-Bopp? Don't people drink, take drugs, or watch porno movies because they want to derive pleasure, and then happiness? Why do people seek God, or any transcendence, if not for the hope of happiness? And let's be honest: We want heaven because we want happiness.

Even the purest acts, at their heart, are usually eudemonistic, that is, their end goal is toward happiness. Did Mother Teresa toil in the slums of India, or Albert Schweitzer in the jungles of Africa, because it made them miserable and they hated every minute of it? Did Oscar Schindler save Jews from the Nazis because doing it made him unhappy? Don't people often act selflessly because they derive satisfaction, even happiness, from the acts themselves? Such examples don't depreciate self-sacrifice, but they show that as fallen human beings, we often, even unconsciously, have happiness as our ultimate aim.

But why not? By seeking happiness, we're seeking what we were originally given in Eden. The quest for happiness is a quest for the essence of humanness. The desire for happiness, of itself, isn't any more evil than the desire for life. The need for happiness is as innate to our nature as is water, even if the latter is usually more accessible.

How ironic, too, that although there's nothing more human than the desire for happiness, few humans have it. "World history is not the basis for happiness," wrote Hegel. "Periods of happiness are blank pages in it."[16]

St. Augustine, understanding well the human condition, wrote in his famous *City of God*:

> This life of ours—if a life so full of such great ills can prop-
> erly be called a life—bears witness to the fact that, from its very
> start, the race of mortal men has been a race condemned. Think,
> first, of the dreadful abyss of ignorance from which all error
> flows and so engulfs the sons of Adam in a darksome pool that
> no one can escape without the toll of toils and tears and fears.
> Then, take our very love for all those things that prove so vain
> and poisonous and breed so many heartaches, troubles, griefs,
> and fears; such insane joys in discord, strife, and wars; such
> fraud and theft and robbery; such perfidy and pride, envy and
> ambition, homicide and murder, cruelty and savagery, lawless-
> ness and lust; all the shameless passions of the impure—forni-
> cation and adultery, incest and unnatural sins, rape and count-
> less other uncleannesses too nasty to be mentioned; the sins
> against religion—sacrilege and heresy, blasphemy and perjury;
> the iniquities against our neighbors—calumnies and cheating,
> lies and false witness, violence to persons and property; the in-
> justices of the courts and the innumerable other miseries and
> maladies that fill the world, yet escape attention.[17]

Sounds like twentieth-century Manhattan, not fifth-century North Africa.

Knowing that man's innermost desire, the end of all his ends, is eudemonistic, Satan has from the beginning placed before us endless roads with neon signs reading "happiness," but which end only in death. Satan uses the superhighways of sex, money, fame, art, power, pride, appetite, even religion, as well as the myriad of small exits breaking off from each one in a tangle of directions that lure billions with false promises of a happiness whose powerful but ambiguous beckoning makes us pathetically easy prey for the bait that we think will satisfy painful wants we can't even identify. Whether seeking happiness through cybersex or the New Age celibacy of Heaven's Gate, whether through gurus or UFOs, through money or power, we can never find what we're looking for because true happiness can be found only in Jesus Christ, who alone can restore us to what we had in Eden.

"For all this hell of unhappiness here on earth," continued St. Augustine, "nothing can save us but the grace of Jesus Christ."[18]

Only Christ can save us because only Christ can get us off the planet. And getting off the planet is the great hope. It's the only hope, because—whether dwelling on the earth for only thirty-one years (like one of the Heaven's Gate cyberpunks who wanted out) or bumbling along the lithosphere for ninety-one years—in the long run, nothing exists for any of us here.

Which is why Christ has promised to take us off the earth and not bring us back until after it has been torn down, purged, then reworked and restored to what had been in the beginning—only better. That's the great truth and promise that "Do" and Company didn't know or understand.

And the one book of the Bible that especially gives us reason to believe, to love, and to relish the promise; the one book that breeds a hope that transcends the innate tragedies of our fallen selves; the one book that constantly calls us to look beyond what we see, hear, and feel and to hope beyond what we know, understand, and expect— comes from the quill of *Yesh-a-ya-hu*, meaning, appropriately enough, "Salvation is of the Lord."

More commonly known as Isaiah, "the gospel prophet."

---

[1]H. L. Mencken, ed., *A New Dictionary of Quotations on Historical Principles From Ancient and Modern Sources* (New York: Alfred Knopf, 1982), 509.
[2]"The Marker We've Been Waiting For," *Time,* April 7, 1997, 31.

[3]Blaise Pascal, "Pensees," *The World's Greatest Thinkers, Man and Spirit: The Speculative Philosophers*, Saxe Commins and Robert N. Liscott, eds. (New York: Random House, 1947), 221.

[4]*Ibid.*, 216.

[5]"The Lure of the Cult," *Time*, April 7, 1997, 45.

[6]Joel Achenbach, "The Outre Limits," *Washington Post,* March 19, 1997, D6.

[7]John Mack, *Abduction: Human Encounters With Aliens* (New York: Charles Scribner's Sons, 1994).

[8]James S. Gordon, "The UFO Experience," *Atlantic Monthly,* August 1991, 88.

[9]John Mack, "Alien Reckoning," *Washington Post,* April 17, 1994, C4.

[10]John Whitehead, "The Search for Meaning and Transcendence," *Rutherford,* October 1996, 13.

[11]Ellen G. White, *Patriarchs and Prophets,* 67.

[12]Immanuel Kant, *Foundations of the Metaphysics of Morals* (Indianapolis: Bobbs-Merrill Educational Publishing, 1980), 35.

[13]Quoted in *American State Papers*, William Addison Blakely, ed. (Hagerstown, Md.: Review and Herald, 1949), 196.

[14]Aristotle, *Nichomachean Ethics* (London: Penguin Classics,1953), 73, 74.

[15]Mortimer Adler, *Ten Philosophical Mistakes* (New York: Collier Books, 1985), 132.

[16]Hegel, quoted in Franz Widemann, *Hegel* (New York: Pegasus Books, 1968), 81.

[17]St. Augustine, *City of God*, Gerald G. Walsh, S. J. trans. (New York: Doubleday &Co., 1958), bk. 22; chap. 22, 519.

[18]*Ibid*, 522.

# T W O

# Final Authority

> *"Sooner or later we all have to accept something as given,
> whether it is God, or logic, or a set of laws,
> or some other foundation of existence."*
> *—mathematical physicist Paul Davies*[1]

When the last brick on the philosophy building at Harvard had been laid, the department wanted this motto, from the pre-Socratic sage Protagoras, to adorn its main wall: "Man is the measure of all things." The president of the prestigious institution, bearing other notions of reality, placed these words there instead: "What is man, that Thou art mindful of him?"

This anecdote is a minor mirror of the great controversy, the cosmic battle between good and evil, light and darkness, Christ and Satan. Despite endless subtle, cryptic, and complicated manifestations, the great controversy can really be pruned down to one sentence: *Who's the creature, who's the Creator, and who's in charge?*

"But you said in your heart, I will ascend above the heavens; to the stars of God I will exalt my throne, and I will sit in the mount of the assembly on the sides of the north. I will ascend to the heights of the clouds. *I will be like the most high"* (Isaiah 14:13, 14).[2]

"Son of man, say to the Prince of Tyrus, Thus saith the Lord God,

Because you have exalted your heart, and you said, *I am God;* I sit in the seat of God in the midst of the seas. But you are man and not God, even if you set your heart as the heart of God. . . . Therefore, thus saith the Lord, because *you set your heart as the heart of God"* (Ezekiel 28:2, 6, italics supplied).

Wrote Ellen White:

> Satan was envious and jealous of Jesus Christ. Yet when all the angels bowed to Jesus to acknowledge his supremacy and high authority and rightful rule, Satan bowed with them; but his heart was filled with envy and hatred. Christ had been taken into the special counsel of God in regard to his plans, while Satan was unacquainted with them. He did not understand, neither was he permitted to know, the purposes of God. But Christ was acknowledged sovereign of Heaven, his power and authority to be the same as that of God himself. Satan thought that he was himself a favorite in Heaven among the angels. He had been highly exalted; but this did not call forth from him gratitude and praise to his Creator. *He aspired to the height of God himself* (italics supplied).[3]

What is it about the creature, even in heavenly and Edenic perfection, that wants to be the Creator, that wants to say in his heart, "I will be like the Most High"? When Satan dangled his lies from a tree in Eden, saying to Eve in her innocence "you will be like God" (Genesis 3:5), she took the bait because, apparently, something inside her wanted to be "like God." Paul, warning about the antichrist wrote:

> "Let no man deceive you by any means: for *that day shall not come*, except there come a falling away first, and that man of sin be revealed, the son of perdition; Who opposeth and exalteth himself above all that is called God, or that is worshipped; so that he as God sitteth in the temple of God, *shewing himself that he is God"* (2 Thessalonians 2:3, 4, italics supplied).

Said theologian Reinhold Niebuhr, "The sin of man is that he seeks to make himself God."[4]

Toward the end of his massive tome, *Being and Nothingness*, French existentialist John Paul Sartre wrote that "the best way to conceive of the fundamental project of human reality is to say that man is a being whose project is to be God. . . . Or if you prefer, man fundamentally is the desire to be God."[5]

Today, with the exception of the New Agers who say that "everybody is God,"[6] and clean-cut Mormons in their white shirts who come to our doors and tell us that we were all once gods and will be again, few have such overt, outward pretensions toward being deity. They don't have to, really, because this "we-are-gods" thing is just one manifestation (a rather crude, blatant one at that) of the real issue, which is—authority. Do we follow the Lord, and let Him be God; or do we make ourselves the final authority—and thus become our own gods?

Eve's words to the serpent in Eden—"but from the fruit of the tree which is in the midst of the garden, God said don't eat from it and don't touch it, lest you die"(Genesis 3:3)—show that, though she knew God's command, she chose another *authority,* in this case her own sense perception ("and the woman saw that the tree was good for food and pleasant to the eyes" [Genesis 3:6]), as well as her own reason, because Satan told Eve that eating from the tree gave him superior knowledge, and she reasoned that she could have that knowledge by doing the same.[7] At the moment of her choice, she tried to become her own god.

Also, Eve wasn't presented with a plethora of possibilities, a parade of options. The garden wasn't a bastion of pluralism, a marketplace of ideas, a Foucaltian "heterotopia."[8] The Eden drama reveals just two authorities in this world, Christ and Satan; Eve, then, had only two choices, all that any of us have, really. And by choosing to obey reason and experience, instead of the command from her Creator, Eve showed who her god really was. However fuzzy, gray, or ambiguous the issues of good and evil, right and wrong, morality and immorality might appear to us now, below the surface, behind the veneer of situational ethics, deontology, Ayn Rand's egoism, Kant's categorical imperative, Bentham's utilitarianism, Thomist moral law, and the endless moral ambiguities that confront us in everyday life—the great controversy is being waged in pure black and white, because there are no shades of gray between Christ and Satan.

The Christian, wrote Ellen White, "should understand the nature of the two principles that are contending for supremacy and should learn to trace their working through the records of history and prophecy, to the great consummation. He should see how this controversy enters into every phase of human experience; how in every act of life he himself reveals the one or the other of the two antagonistic motives; and how, whether he will or not, he is even now deciding upon which side of the controversy he will be found."[9]

Eden proves that, at the most fundamental level, a moral middle ground is impossible. Eve had to choose; so do we. Her decision proved her loyalties; ours do too. She couldn't be neutral; we can't either.

For any human being the crucial questions are, What is the final, authoritative source of our knowledge? When conflicting data, ideas, and concepts appear, which one do we believe and follow? To whose drum do we march, because we always march to someone's?

Given the nature of reality, we answer these questions by what we believe, say, and do. And regardless of all the manifold ways it may appear to us in the phenomenal world—in the world we see and experience with sense, reason, and thought—we're under one authority or another. Which one we accept is our own choice; what we *don't* have a choice in is the act itself of deciding. "Choose you this day," commanded Joshua, "whom you will serve" (Joshua 24:15), because (as Bob Dylan sang) "You gotta serve someone."

For centuries, this battle over whom we serve was relatively simple—at least in the Christian West. God was on His throne in heaven, and man was to worship and obey Him. The great controversy revealed itself mostly in *how* the Lord was to be worshiped and obeyed. The theological struggles—whether among "Aphtharto-docetists, Corrupticolists and Theopaschitists,"[10] or the religious violence of the Thirty Years' War—were, essentially, over authority. Was God going to be worshiped and served as He commanded, showing that He was the ultimate authority; or were men going to do it their own way, showing, in the end, that their final authority, their god, was themselves and their institutions (i.e., Satan)?

Over time, however, as the Western world began moving away from a monolithic, theo-centered worldview to one more humanistic, diverse, and less dogmatic, the issue became more complicated. Under the centrifugal force of the Renaissance, the Enlightenment, and the scientific revolution—axioms, first principles, and fundamentals on which a thousand years of Western civilization rested, cracked or were swept away. A powerful, crucial break started to be made between nature and nature's God, with an emphasis on the former until the latter became relegated to the realm of myth, irrational metaphysical speculation, and "hypothesis" (an unprovable one at that). Mankind moved, as Auguste Comte wrote, "through three different theoretical conditions: the Theological . . . the Metaphysical . . . the Scientific."[11] Truth, in a sense, was pulled out of heaven, out of the realm of theology and transcendent metaphysics, and lodged, instead, on earth, to be found only in nature (science), man (anthropology), and mind (psychology).

"Science replaced religion," wrote Richard Tarnas, "as preeminent intellectual *authority*, as definer, judge, and guardian of the cultural worldview. Human reason and empirical observation [what Satan used on Eve in Eden] replaced theological doctrine and scriptural revelation as the principal means for comprehending the universe. The domains of religion and metaphysics became gradually compartmentalized, regarded as personal, subjective, speculative, and fundamentally distinct from public objective knowledge and the empirical world. Faith and reason were now definitely severed" (italics supplied).[12]

Advertently or inadvertently, when men like William of Ockham and Dun Scotus drove a "wedge between philosophy and theology, and faith and reason,"[13] when Copernicus uprooted centuries of "Christian" cosmology by disproving a geocentric universe, when Newton showed that creation wasn't so mysterious but in fact worked by set laws like a machine, when Kant postulated the limits of our rational minds to understand God, when Fichte put all truth in the "ego," when Nietzsche argued that God is dead and there are no facts, only opinions, when Darwin theorized that we were products of blind naturalistic forces, when William James said that truth is whatever works, and when Heisenberg showed there was very little determinacy to anything—step by step man's ties to the transcendent, to any overarching metaphysical truth, much less to a personal loving God, became unmoored until man found himself alone in a cold cosmic void, with truth being only what he makes it.

Thus, the great controversy is now being fought, not so much over how to worship God, but over whether God even exists, or if He does, how we can know anything about Him. Truth has been demoted. It's now lodged, not in an eternal, cosmic transcendence, but only in man himself, in his own notions, rules, and predilections, either individually or as a community. "Truth," wrote jurist Robert Bork, "is what the majority thinks it is at any given moment precisely because the majority is permitted to govern and redefine its values constantly."[14]

Yet by severing ties with the transcendent, by cutting away the theological dimension of a two-tiered reality, so that only the natural tier remains—man has come to the point where, if there is to be hope, it must be found in himself, in whatever values, truths, and meaning he can derive from existence through "human reason and empirical observation" because there's nothing else above, no deity to reveal it to him. Humanity alone erects the pillars of justice; we alone name good and evil; we alone create rules; we alone determine values. Truth comes from within rather than from without—much less from above. We become, like Eve in Eden, our own gods.

In short, however vastly more complicated it might appear on the surface, the great controversy in the last century of this millennium is the same as it was in Eden millennia ago: We want to be "like God."

But we're not. We're not even close, and, in fact, the harder we try to be like God the less like Him we become. We can be compared to people who—thinking they can get where they want to go by swimming rather than sailing—jump ship and, finding the water too deep and rough, cling only to each other in hope of staying afloat. We've rooted truth only in ourselves, and because we're weak, vacillating, fearful, evanescent, unstable, and sinking, our truths are weak, vacillating, fearful, evanescent, unstable, and sinking as well. By severing ourselves from God, man has only himself left, a prospect that—as this century disappears into the next—becomes increasingly more depressing.

Wrote Peter Martin:

> The great drama at the heart of modern American secularism has always been that religion would slowly wither away, giving way, as it did so, to reason, to a morality rooted not in a fear of God or the hope of heaven but in reflection, a sense of kinship, and a belief in the common good. Values once maintained through oppression or fear would rise naturally through human reason, instinct, sympathy. The religious divisions and hatred separating us from one another would disappear, and the sense of gratitude and awe traditionally felt for God would be transferred to the human world and provide a foundation for a universalized community. As we know, none of this came to be, nor is it likely to come to be. The struggle to live ethically without God has left us not with the just and moral order we imagined but with disorder and confusion.[15]

Modern secularism has brought us to an abyss as empty, unstable, and shallow as the human ego. The more we lift ourselves up, the lower we fall; the more we learn about the world, the less we know how to cope with it; the deeper into the atom we go, the more lost we become; the more we communicate, the less we hear. Humanity hasn't gotten better, only more efficient in its ignorance—even to the point where, rather than simply casting off the dogmatic certainty of theological orthodoxy, it has so untethered objectivity from any solid foundation that it has rejected even the concept of "truth" itself. In any form, be it theological, metaphysical, or even natural, the very idea of "truth" is denied. This is the era of post-modernism, where such concepts as truth and morality, right and wrong, even up and down, don't exist in any objective, absolute sense but only as relative, indeterminate, and fluctuating notions that each individual and community must define for itself. Unlike the modern world's belief in an objective reality that could be understood by human reason—post-modernism rejects the very notion of objectivity itself, a position that inevitably leads to moral chaos.[16]

One recent and embarrassing example of the emptiness, helplessness, and silly ignorance of post-modernism occurred when, as a joke, physicist Alan Sokal submitted to the scholarly journal *Social Texts* a ridiculously titled article, "Transgressing the Boundaries: Toward a Transformative Hermeneutics of Quantum Gravity" (come on, a *hermeneutics* of quantum gravity!?). Yet, amazingly enough, the article—filled with arcane and abstract silliness, including phrases such as "emancipatory mathematics" and "liberatory science"—was published as a serious piece.

"What does this say," asked Peter Berkowitz in the *New Republic,* "about the state of academic life that leading scholars were unable to distinguish serious argument from utter nonsense."[17]

It says that when man chooses the wrong side in the great controversy, when he chooses to be his own god and to make himself his own authority, he wallows, not only in emptiness, meaninglessness, and death but in ignorance and nonsense as well. It says that man seeking truth only in himself, through his own reason, experience, and imagination, can never know anything other than what his own limited, subjective, fallen, and erroneous reason, experience, and imagination can show him—which isn't much. It says that if man wants truth, he needs to get it from an authority higher, less subjective, and less limited than himself—One that would know, for instance, that you can't do hermeneutics on quantum gravity and that "emancipatory mathematics" is a joke!

No doubt, that authority—the only other authority in the universe—is the Lord, and He reveals truth through the Holy Scriptures, the sole source that can get us beyond the blinders that reason, experience, intuition, culture, and tradition have placed on us in a reality so complicated that one can prove "the simple fact that $a \times b \neq b \times a$."[18] The Bible is the only objective standard for helping us decode a world that unfolds itself to fallen humanity as "a bloomin' buzzing confusion." The Bible alone can lift us from the blind back alleys and ridiculous dead ends of humanistic rationalism, empiricism, and naturalism to the transcendent, living God, the One in whom "we live, and move, and have our being" (Acts 17:28). As St. Augustine wrote to the Lord in his *Confessions:* "And so, since we are too weak to discover the truth by reason alone and for this reason need the authority of the sacred books, I began to believe that you would never have invested the Bible with such conspicuous authority in every land unless you had intended it to be the means by which we should look for you and believe in you."[19]

The Word is the only way we can know, for sure, that we're not the *subject* of truth but the *object* of truth, that we're not the *determiners* of truth but the *consequences*, not the *creators* of truth but the *recipients* of it.

One can argue, however, that we bring our own subjectivity to the Bible. After all, why are there so many denominations—each with its own view of truth even though all claim to derive that view from the same source—if not for human subjectivity? That's true, to a degree, but still the essentials of salvation, including "the commandments of God and the faith of Jesus" (Revelation 14:12), are taught clearly enough in Scripture to transcend the otherwise impossible locks that our sinful nature—mixed with culture, hormones, genes, and education—has clamped on our minds. In short, under the guidance of the Holy Spirit, a seeker can learn enough objective truth from the Bible to know the answers to the crucial questions: *Who's the creature, who's the Creator, and who's in charge?*

And that's the exact reason why Satan tries to keep us from the Bible or, even more specifically, from the truths revealed in it. In the old days, Roman inquisitors suited his purpose well; today, higher criticism works even better. Applying the methods, presuppositions, and ideologies of modern, atheistic naturalism, higher criticism is Bible interpretation premised on the notion that truth resides, not in heaven, but in man—and that man, as god, is the final arbiter of truth, morality, and law. The higher critical method is one of the latest, and most dangerous (not to mention arrogant), manifestations of what first did us in at Eden—man playing God. In a less theological sphere, higher criticism is, basically, humanity lowering the eternal, transcendent verities of Scripture to its own level, akin to turning the *Mona Lisa* into a *Hustler* magazine foldout.

Of course, it's one thing to bring atheistic, rationalistic, and naturalist presuppositions to science, sociology, or anthropology; to some degree, such an approach succeeds. But to bring to the Bible a method of interpretation premised on the beliefs that there is no God, no supernatural, no transcendent reality, is like doing math without symbols, physics without matter, or zoology without animals.

Higher criticism (be it form criticism, source criticism, the historical-critical method, or redaction criticism) starts from the assumption that "God's Word" is really man's word cloaked as God's, and thus every act of higher criticism itself is a denial of God's Word *as God's Word*. It assumes that Scripture, if not a book of outright lies, was composed by ignorant ancients trapped in the myths and mysteries of their era. Those who argue that they can apply higher critical methods without accepting higher critical assumptions fool themselves. In higher criticism, *the method itself* is the message. In the end, higher criticism tells us only about ourselves; it reveals nothing about God.

How could it? When the secularist, rationalist premises of modernity were applied to the natural world, it gave humanity something as hopeless, meaningless, empty—and wrong!—as mechanistic evolution. When applied to the Bible, it gives the same hopeless, meaningless, empty, and wrong answers. It has to, because the higher critical method takes the promises, the hopes, the cosmic entelechies of Scripture—the essence of what the book is about and the eternal objective truths of reality—and turns them into nothing but man-made myths that (according to Rudolph Bultmann) do not "present an objective picture of the world as it is, but . . . express man's understanding of himself in the world in which he lives."[20] In other words, the Bible isn't the expression of an eternal, omniscient, powerful God, but only the thoughts of subjective, fleeting, fearful men trying to grasp the world around them. Thus, going no higher than man, centering all truth in man, making man the creator of truth itself, higher criticism offers nothing more than man—which is why, in the end, it leads only to futility, contradiction, meaninglessness, and death. Ultimately this is all that man has on his own. And, in few places is the nihilistic destructiveness of higher criticism, as well as its vacuity and incoherence, better revealed than in what such an approach has done with the book of Isaiah.

Isaiah presents a problem to the secular presuppositions of higher criticism: How could a book written in the eighth century B.C. predict events in the sixth century B.C., even mentioning, by name, the ruler who would liberate the Jews from Babylonian captivity?

"Who says to *Cyrus,* he is my shepherd, and all my desire he will complete. . . . Thus saith the Lord to His anointed, to *Cyrus,* whose right hand I have made strong" (Isaiah 44:28; 45:1, italics supplied).

Isaiah names "Cyrus," and if we accept what Isaiah says about himself—that he ministered in the reigns of "Uzziah, Jotham, Ahaz, *and* Hezekiah, kings of Judah" (Isaiah 1:1)—his ministry in Jerusalem would extend from about "750 B.C. to 700 B.C.,"[21] though possibly a decade or so longer. Cyrus, however, doesn't get involved in Jewish history until the mid-sixth century, which means that Isaiah named him at least a century and a half earlier.

From a historical-critical perspective, however, people can't make such accurate predictions more than a century before the events. So the higher critics claim that another Isaiah, "the Second Isaiah" (or "the Deutero-Isaiah"), who lived more than a century and a half after the first, is the one who wrote the part of the book that names Cyrus (usually seen as beginning with chapter 40). Some higher critics even claim there was a "third Isaiah" (the "trito-Isaiah"). This idea was made prominent by J. C. Doderlein (1789) who "argued on rationalistic grounds that an Isaiah of the eighth century could neither foresee two centuries ahead to the fall of Jerusalem and the exile nor could he have foretold the rise of Cyrus 150 years before he appeared on the scene of history."[22]

That position, however, blatantly contradicts what Isaiah itself says about the power of God to predict the future:

> Have you not heard from long ago that I have done it, and that from ancient times I have formed it? Now I have brought it to pass, and it will be. . . . Behold, the former things have come to pass; and new things I have declared; before they spring forth I will declare them to you. . . . And who, like me, will call and declare it, and set it in order for me. . . . Have not I, from long ago, proclaimed it to you, and declared it . . . ? Who has proclaimed these from ancient times; from long ago declared it . . . ? Remember the former things from long ago and that I am God and there are no other gods and none like me, declaring from

the beginning latter things, and from ancient times things that had not yet been done, saying, My counsel will stand and I will do all my pleasure. . . . Yea, I have spoken, and I will bring it to pass, I have formed it, and also, I will do it. . . . From earlier times I have declared the former things; and from my mouth they went forth. And I proclaimed them; suddenly, I did them, and they came to pass. . . . Long ago, I declared them to you. Before they came to pass I proclaimed them to you, lest you should say, my idol, and my graven image, and my molten image commanded them (Isaiah 37:26; 40:28; 41:22, 23; 42:8, 9; 44:7, 8; 45:11; 45:21; 46:9-11; 48:3; 48:5).

God says He can predict the future; the higher critics say He can't, and they have built a whole structure on that premise. Whom does one believe? The answer, of course, depends upon who is one's God.

The higher critical approach also runs into another, even more fundamental, problem: Isaiah's predictions of Christ. Even if one accepted a sixth-century Isaiah, how did the prophet in chapter 53 so accurately predict the sufferings of Jesus more than half a millennium later?

Their answer, the only one open to them (given their narrow, parochial premises) is to deny that Isaiah 53, or any of "the Servant songs," refer to Christ. Writing about the "venerable belief in the Christian church" that these songs, especially Isaiah 53, "are predictions of Jesus Christ," John L. McKenzie said "this opinion is defended by no one today except in a few fundamentalist circles. This type of predicative prophecy does not appear in the Old Testament."[23]

Predicative prophecy in the Old Testament? How silly!

Instead of Jesus, the Suffering Servant in Isaiah 53 has been identified as everyone from "Zerubabbel . . . Jehoaichin . . . [or] Moses."[24] John D. W. Watts links the character in Isaiah 53 to Persian King Darius.[25] R. N. Whybray writes that the chapter was probably written by friends of the prophet about the prophet himself.[26] Old Testament scholar William Holladay, meanwhile, reiterated another common view of Isaiah 53—that it's talking about the nation of Israel, or that the writer "may have had a representative group within Israel itself in mind."[27]

What these positions mean, of course, is that John (12:38), Matthew (8:17), Paul (Romans 10:16), Philip (Acts 8:32, 33), and Peter (1 Peter 2:24)—who, though quoting various parts of Isaiah, make no distinctions between a first, second, and third prophet—were wrong in their interpretation of Isaiah 53 as containing predictions of Christ and His work. And if these New Testament authors were wrong on something so fundamental as the identity of Jesus from the Old Testament, why trust anything else they write about Him? How accurate, for example, is Luke's account of Christ in the synagogue (chapter 4), where Jesus specifically applies the prophecy of Isaiah 61 to Himself? And, given the higher critical premises, how could Jesus have been right in applying to Himself something written centuries earlier?

"Man can be exalted," wrote Ellen White, "only by laying hold of the merits of a crucified and risen Saviour. The finest intellect, the most exalted position will not secure heaven. Satan had the highest education that could be obtained. This education he received under the greatest of all teachers. When men talk of higher criticism; when they pass their judgment upon the word of God, call their attention to the fact that they have forgotten who was the first and wisest critic. He has had thousands of years of practical experience. He it is who teaches the so-called higher critics of the world today. God will punish all those who, as higher critics, exalt themselves, and criticize God's Holy word."[28]

The emptiness of the higher critical technique, and the startling errors it must inevitably lead to, is epitomized by the highly-publicized Jesus Seminar, in which a group of New Testament scholars attempted to discern from the Gospels which statements of Jesus were authentic and which weren't. The seminar concluded that only "18 per cent of the words ascribed to Jesus in the Gospels may have actually been spoken by him. John was eliminated completely. Only one sentence in Mark met muster."[29] The Virgin birth, the resurrection of Christ, all the miracles, the seminar said, were fabricated. The Gospels themselves "must be seen as the product of authors who never met Jesus, relied on second- and third-generation stories, and can't be counted on to quote him correctly."[30] Their scholarship came to the interesting conclusion, too, that Jesus wasn't resurrected from the dead, but that dogs ate His corpse after the crucifixion, which explains the empty tomb.

What a brilliant, objective conclusion! They might as well have concluded that a UFO took Him to Hale-Bopp (which would be closer to the truth). Instead of a risen Savior now ministering in our behalf in the heavenly sanctuary, as Scripture teaches, higher criticism gives us one whose body was scarfed down by a bunch of hungry mutts. Of course! Once truth becomes unmoored from any metaphysical transcendence and is lodged instead only in human subjectivity and man's skewed notions of rationality and reality, anything goes. When man, as Protagoras wrote, is the "measure of all things," then all things, especially truth, become distorted, even lost—and nothing better exemplifies this distortion than what the Jesus Seminar has done to "the Truth" Himself. And without "the Truth," what do we have?

The answer, perhaps, was best expressed in 1882, by Frederich Nietzsche's famous passage:

Have you not heard of that madman who lit a lantern in the bright morning hours, ran to the market place and cried incessantly: "I am looking for God! I am looking for God!"—As many of those who did not believe in God were standing together there he excited considerable laughter. "Have you lost him then?" said one. "Did he lose his way like a child?" said another. "Or is he hiding? Is he afraid of us? Has he gone on a voyage? or emigrated?"—thus they shouted and laughed. The madman sprang into their midst and pierced them with his glances. "Where has God gone?" he cried. "I shall tell you. *We have killed him*—you and I. We are all his murderers. But how have we done this? How were we able to drink up the sea? Who gave us the sponge to wipe away the entire horizon? What did we do when we unchained this earth from its sun? Whither is it moving now? Whither are we moving now? Away from all suns? Are we not perpetually falling? Backward, sideward, forward, in all directions? Is there any up or down left? Are we not straying as through an infinite nothing? Do we not feel the breath of empty space? Has it not become colder? Is more and more night not coming on all the time? Must not lanterns be lit in the morning? Do we not hear anything yet of the noise of the grave-diggers who are burying God? Do we not smell anything yet of God's decomposition?—gods too decompose. God is dead. God remains dead. And we have killed him. How shall we, the murderers of all murderers, console ourselves? That which was holiest and mightiest of all that the world has yet possessed has bled to death under our knives— who will wipe this blood off us? With what water could we purify ourselves? What festivals of atonement, what sacred games shall we need to invent? Is not the greatness of this deed too great for us? *Must not we ourselves become gods simply to seem worthy of it?*"[31] (italics supplied).

Nietzsche is saying that, having lost our tie to the transcendent, to God (the ultimate transcendence) whom we have killed, we are unmoored from anything stable. The earth, as it were, has been "unchained . . . from its sun," and thus we are moving away "from all suns . . . perpetually falling . . . backward, sideward, forward, in all directions." The madman asked if we must "become gods to seem worthy" of such a task? The answer is that, since Eden, we have already tried to make ourselves gods, which is why we've been severed from the only true God.

And a contemporary manifestation of that role reversal is the post-

Enlightenment, post-modernist rejection of the two-tiered reality revealed in Scripture. Existence is limited to the tunnel vision of naturalism, materialism, and rationalism, an exceedingly narrow perspective. "I don't know about God," wrote German novelist Gunther Grass. "The only things I know are what I see, hear, feel, and smell."[32] Thus, he must—by the absolute nature of reality—know so pathetically little. Thomas Jefferson, the paragon of reason, once unwittingly showed just how limited this view is when he wrote: "Of all of the gifts of heaven to man, it is next to the most precious, if it be not the most precious."[33]

And what was this "most precious" heavenly gift, according to Jefferson? The Scriptures? The atonement? The promise of Christ's return?

No. The olive tree!

Heaven, fortunately, is much more generous and broad than Jefferson's rational mind allowed, and among heaven's most precious gifts to man are not only the incredible promises of a redone, remade, and totally new world, but the powerful reasons to believe those promises—reasons to trust, to hope, to know with certainty that God is going to do for us what we could never do for ourselves and, in fact, what we can't even imagine ever being done at all.

But to claim those promises we must believe them, and to believe them we must first break the earthen shackles that contemporary Western culture, tradition, education, and thought have clamped on our minds. Ever since Descartes, we have been focused downward, even inward, for answers to the questions that relentlessly pull at our hair. *Rolling Stone* magazine, in an article about Beat Generation icon Allen Ginsberg, exemplified this trend by saying that the term "Beat" came to stand for "an idea that to discover one's true self and the self's liberation, you first had to descend into some of the most secret, used-up, and bereft parts of your heart, soul, body, and consciousness."[34] Yet descending inward is exactly where you don't go, because that is exactly where truth doesn't reside, which is why many (not just Beatniks) have come to the hopeless, nihilistic conclusion that truth doesn't exist at all.

Instead, we must reach up, outward, and beyond what we can perfectly see, understand, or measure because that's where the truth is. We must get beyond what this world offers because what it offers is transient, fleeting, always passing away—and truth, by its very nature as truth, must be eternal. The most important truth of all reality is the truth about Jesus, a truth that we could never discover on our own.

Whatever humans do, we always begin from wherever we are—and so this book (no exception) begins from the premise that the man-centered, post-modernistic worldview is just another manifestation of Satan's lie to Eve in Eden, and that concepts such as a first, second, and third Isaiah (and the entire higher critical project) are specific examples of that same old lie. This book assumes that the Bible is God's view of Himself and man, and not man's view of himself and God. This book assumes that the hope Scripture presents is as true as God Himself, and that the hard questions in the Bible don't need to be answered in order for us to trust its promises any more than we need to understand the hard questions about thermo-nuclear fusion in order to be warmed by the sun. As Peter Davies said, "sooner or later we all have to accept something as given," and this book is premised on the "given" that the Bible provides the sole truly objective view of the world.

"Only a God," said Martin Heidegger, "can save us,"[35] and this book's final assumption is that the only God who can do so is the true One, revealed through the writing of Isaiah, the One who through His Word has answered the crucial questions: *Who's the creature, who's the Creator, and who's in charge?*

-----

[1]Paul Davies, *The Mind of God: The Scientific Basis for a Rational World* (New York: Simon & Schuster, 1992), 15.

[2]Unless otherwise indicated, all Hebrew and Aramaic translations have been done by the author.

[3]*Spirit of Prophecy*, 1:18.

[4]Reinhold Neibuhr, *The Nature and Destiny of Man, vol. 1, Human Nature* (New York: Charles Scribner's Sons, 1964), 140.

[5]John Paul Sartre, *Being and Nothingness: A Phenomenological Essay on Ontology* (New York: Washington Square Press, 1956), 724.

[6]"New Age Harmonies," *Time,* December 7, 1987, 64.

[7]"The tempter assured Eve that as soon as she ate of the fruit she would receive a new and superior knowledge that would make her equal with God. He called her attention to himself. He ate freely of the tree and found it not only perfectly harmless, but delicious and exhilarating; and told her that it was because of its wonderful properties to impart wisdom and power that God had prohibited them from tasting or even touching it; for he knew its wonderful qualities. He stated that by eating of the fruit of the tree forbidden them was the reason he had attained the power of speech." *Spirit of Prophecy,* 1:37, 38.

[8]Michael Foucalt, *The Order of Things: An Archaeology of the Human Sciences* (New York: Pantheon Books, 1970), xviii.

[9]*Education,* 90.

[10]J. M. Roberts, *History of the World* (Middlesex: Penguin Books, 1983), 339.

[11]Auguste Comte, *The Positive Philosophy,* excerpted in *The World's Great Thinkers: The Philosophers of Science* (New York: Random House, 1947), 219.

[12]Richard Tarnas, *The Passion of the Western Mind* (New York: Ballantine Books, 1991), 234.

[13]Samuel Enoch Strumpf, *Socrates to Sartre* (New York: McGraw-Hill, 1982), 189.

[14]Robert Bork, "Neutral Principles and Some First Amendment Problems," *The Normative Constitution: Essays for the Third Century,* Richard Sherlock, Kent Robson, Charles Johnson, eds. (Lanham, Md.: Rowman and Littlefield Publishers, 1995), 37.

[15]Peter Marin, *Freedom and Its Discontents: Reflection on Four Decades of American Moral Experience* (Steerforth Press), quoted in "Secularism's Blind Faith," *Harper's Magazine*, September 1995, 20.

[16]"For twenty-five hundred years," wrote Houston Smith, "philosophers have argued over which metaphysical system is true. For them to agree that none is true is a new departure." But the post-modernist premise is self-defeating. After all, if *anything* exists—then truth (the explanation, purpose, and meaning of that existence) must exist as well. Even if there were only "nothingness," truth (why this "nothingness" instead of something?) would still have to exist. To deny the reality of truth is, *a priori*, self-contradictory; the denial itself refutes its own assertion. For truth to be denied, something has to exist to deny it, and thus truth must exist as well. Nevertheless, however ludicrous, contradictory, untenable, and extreme the position, this is where man, having severed himself from the true God and put himself in God's role instead, has wound up—in utter self-contradiction. "I would give my life for a man who is looking for truth," said dadaist Luis Bunuel. "But I would gladly kill a man who thinks that he has found the truth" (Bunuel obviously believed strongly enough in the "truth" to believe that whoever claimed to have truth should die).

[17]Peter Berkowitz, "Science Fiction: Postmodernism Exposed," *The New Republic,* July 1, 1996, 15.

[18]John Gribbin, *In Search of Schrodinger's Cat: Quantum Physics and Reality* (New York: Bantam Books, 1984), 139.

[19]St. Augustine, *Confessions*, R. S. Pine-Coffin, trans. (London: Penguin Books, 1961), 117.

[20]Rudolph Bultmann, *Kerygma and Myth*, quoted in Colin Brown, *Philosophy & the Christian Faith* (Downer's Grove, Ill.: InterVarsity Press, 1968), 187.

[21]John D. W. Watts, *Isaiah 1-33* (*Word Biblical Commentary*) (Waco: Word Books, 1985), xxv.

[22]Gerhard Hasel, *Biblical Interpretation Today* (Washington, D.C.: Biblical Research Institute, 1985), 29.

[23]John L. McKenzie, *Second Isaiah* (The Anchor Bible) (New York: Doubleday & Co. 1983), xlix.

[24]Eissfeldt, Otto, *The Old Testament: An Introduction* (New York: Harper and Row, 1965), 334.

[25]John D. W. Watts, *Isaiah 34-66* (*Word Bible Commentary*) (Waco: Word Books, 1987), 230.

[26]"In Isa. 53," Whybray explains, "the allusiveness of the language does not permit us to say precisely what was the occasion of this giving of thanks, but it may be surmised that it was the release of Deutero-Isaiah from a Babylonian prison, where he had been subjected to the sufferings of which the third 'Servant Song' (50:4-9) also speaks. The reason for his release is not known; but it would appear that his friends took it as a miracle and as a sign that the tide of their sufferings had turned, and that the deliverance of the exiles was about to begin. This, together with his exalted role as the bearer of Yahweh's word, would account for the exalted language in which they speak of him." Whybray, R. N. *Isaiah 40-66: The New Century Bible Commentary* (Grand Rapids, Mich.: Wm. B. Eerdmans, 1990), 172.

[27]William Holladay, *Isaiah: Scroll of a Prophetic Heritage* (Grand Rapids, Mich.: Wm. B. Eerdmans, 1978), 158.

[28]*Review and Herald*, March 16, 1897.

[29]David Van Biema, "The Gospel Truth?" *Time*, April 8, 1996, 56.

[30]Mark O'Keefe, "Was—and Is—Jesus Divine? Scholars Clash Over His Identity," *Religious News Service*, February 7, 1996, 7.

[31]Frederick Nietzsche, *The Gay Science* (1882 edition, 125) excerpted from Walter Kaufmann, *The Portable Nietzsche* (New York: Viking Press, 1954), 93.

[32]Gunther Grass, quoted in *Paris Herald Tribune*, March 23, 1970.

[33]Quoted in Dumas Malone, *Jefferson and His Time: Jefferson and the Rights of Man* (Boston: Little, Brown, and Company, 1951), 127.

[34]Mikal Gilmore, "Allen Ginsburg: 1926–1997," *Rolling Stone*, May 29, 1997, 38.

[35]Martin Heidegger, "Only a God Can Save Us: The Spiegel Interview," in *Heidegger: The Man and the Thinker* (Chicago: Precedent Publishing, 1966), 45.

# THREE

# Origins
# Matter

*"The chief business of all philosophy consists in solving
the problem of the existence of the world."*
*—Fredrich von Schelling[1]*

Philosopher Bertrand Russell, the story goes, had just lectured on the orbits of the planets around the sun, and the orbit of the sun around the center of the galaxy, when an old lady in black tennis shoes rose and said that the earth was a flat disc sitting on the back of a turtle. Russell, jesting, asked what the turtle sat on, and she responded that it sat on another turtle. "Ma'am," Russell continued joking, "what then does *that* turtle sit on?" She answered, "Another turtle," but before he could ask what that turtle sat on, she wagged her finger in his face and snapped, "Save your breath, sonny, it's turtles all the way down."

However cute, that story deals with *the* most crucial issue of human existence—the nature of the universe itself. To be sure, most people aren't overtly preoccupied with the questions that Lucasian Professor of Mathematics Stephen Hawking at Cambridge (Isaac Newton's old job) asked in *A Brief History of Time:* "What do we know about the universe, and how do we know it? Where did the universe come from, and where is it going? Did the universe have a beginning, and if so, what happened *before* then?"[2]

Nevertheless, these questions aren't only about quasars, black holes, and string theory; they're about ourselves, about who we are, why we're here, and about the meaning of our lives. We are, after all, part of the universe, so truth about it involves truth about us.

"As our fate is totally dependent upon that matrix that produced and sustained us," wrote Houston Smith, "interest in its nature is the holiest interest that can visit us."[3]

He's right. Origins matter, even greatly, because only in our origins can we discover the true cause, purpose, and meaning of our lives.[4] Origins, in fact, are more about the present and the future than about the past, because our view of where we came from will affect our view of where we're going, why, and how we'll act until we get there.

Wrote Bertrand Russell:

> That man is the product of causes which had no prevision of the end they were achieving, that his origin, his growth, his hopes and fears, his loves and his beliefs, are but the outcome of accidental collocations of atoms; that no fire, no heroism, no intensity of thought and feeling, can preserve an individual life beyond the grave; that all the noonday brightness of human genius, are destined to extinction in the vast death of the solar system, and that the whole temple of Man's achievement must inevitably be buried beneath the debris of a universe in ruins—all these things, if not quite beyond dispute, are yet so nearly certain that no philosophy which rejects them can hope to stand. Only within the scaffolding of these truths, only on the firm foundation of unyielding despair, can the soul's habitation henceforth be safely built.[5]

A person who sees himself as only "an accidental collation of atoms" will, no doubt, live differently from one who sees himself as part of the grand overarching purpose of God. Belief in any theological cosmology (Hindu, Muslim, Hebrew, Christian, whatever) will give a person a perspective that must influence his actions to one degree or another, for better or for worse (after all, Hezbollah suicide bombers believe in a purposeful Creator too). A Hindu will think twice before doing whatever he does, if he believes that whatever he does determines whether he's reincarnated as a fruit fly or a Brahman. A Christian who believes that "God shall bring every work into judgment with every secret thing, whether it be good, or whether it be evil" (Ecclesiastes 12:14) will, to some degree, act differently than a person whose concept of origins doesn't allow for a final, divine judgment.

Origins matter, even greatly, which is why Isaiah talks so much about them.

> Lift up high your eyes, and see who has created these things, who has brought forth by number their host; He has called all of them by name; from the multitude of His strength and the might of His power not one fails. . . . The Lord of hosts, the God of Israel, dwells on the cherubim; you alone are the Lord of all the kingdoms of the earth. You have made the heavens and the earth. . . . Have you not known, have you not heard, the Lord is the everlasting God, the Creator of the ends of the earth. . . . Thus says the Lord God, the one who created the heavens and stretched them out; He hammered out the earth and those that came from it. He gives breath to the people on it, and spirit to them that walk on it. . . . And now, thus says the Lord, your Creator, Jacob, and the one who formed you, Israel. . . . Thus says the Lord, your Redeemer and who formed you from the womb, I am the Lord, who has made all things, stretching out the heavens, spreading out the earth. . . . I have made the earth, and I, even I, have created man upon it. My hands stretched forth the heavens, and all their host I have commanded. . . . Thus says the Lord, who created the heavens, He is God, who formed the earth, and made it. He established it not in vain; He created it to be inhabited. I formed it and there is no other. . . . Also, my hand laid the foundations of the earth and my right hand spread

out heaven. When I call them, they stand up together" (Isaiah
40:26; 37:16; 40:28; 42:5; 43:1; 44:24; 45:12; 45:18; 48:13).

These are just a smattering of the rich and varied verses in Isaiah
that unequivocally point to the Lord as the cause of all that is caused.
Isaiah is suffused with the Creation theme, as if each syllable in Genesis 1:1 contained a canopy of truth to be released later from Isaiah
in words profuse with purpose, hope, and promise for those broad-
minded and blessed enough to believe them.

In fact, the word *created* (*bara*) in Genesis 1:1 appears in the Old
Testament almost fifty times, with Isaiah using it far more than any other
prophet. *Bara*, which means "to shape, fashion, create," appears only in
the context of divine activity: it denotes the work of God alone. *Bara* "is
a special verb in the OT [Old Testament]. It always has God as its subject; it is never used of human activity. You and I may make, form, or
fashion, but only God creates."[6] And, in one form or another, Isaiah uses
*bara* seventeen times, more than twice as often as Genesis itself.

It's not just Isaiah. From the words of Moses 1,300 years before
Christ, to the words of John in the decades following Him, the Word is
unambiguous about origins. In one style or another, in one context or
another, through one prophet or another, the Scripture expresses with an
algebraic consistency the theme that, far from mankind being an "accidental collation of atoms," human origins are rooted in the purposeful
act of God, who created us with premeditation and foresight.

These are the generations of the heavens and the earth, when
they were created, in the day the Lord God made heaven and
earth (Genesis 2:4).

For in six days God made the heavens and the earth, the sea,
and all which is in them (Exodus 20:11).

Huram said, Blessed be the Lord God of Israel, who made

the heavens and the earth (2 Chronicles 2:12).

Know that the Lord, He is God; He made us, and not we ourselves (Psalm 100:3).

You are blessed of the Lord, who made the heavens and the earth (Psalm 115:15).

For behold, He formed the mountains and created the wind, and declared to man what are his thoughts (Amos 4:13).

You are the Lord alone; you have made the heavens, the heavens of heaven and all their host, the earth and all which is upon it; the seas, and all that is in them (Nehemiah 9:6).

Have not we one Father, has not one God created us? (Malachi 2:10).

But from the beginning of the creation, God "made them male and female" (Mark 10:6, NKJV).

And to make all people see what is the fellowship of the mystery, which from the beginning of the ages has been hidden in God who created all things through Jesus Christ (Ephesians 3:9, NKJV).

For by Him [Jesus Christ] all things were created that are in heaven and that are on earth, visible and invisible, whether thrones or dominions or principalities or powers. All things were created through Him and for Him. And He is before all things, and in Him all things consist (Colossians 1:16, 17, NKJV).

You, Lord, in the beginning laid the foundation of the earth, And the heavens are the works of Your hands (Hebrews 1:10, NKJV).

And swore by Him who lives forever and ever, who created heaven and the things that are in it, the earth and the things that are in it, and the sea and the things that are in it, that there should be delay no longer (Revelation 10:6, NKJV).

You are worthy, O Lord, To receive glory and honor and power; For You created all things, and by your will they exist and were created (Revelation 4:11, NKJV).

Then I saw another angel flying in the midst of heaven . . . saying with a loud voice, "Fear God, and give glory to Him, for the hour of His judgment has come; and worship Him who made heaven and earth, the sea and springs of water" (Revelation 14:6, 7, NKJV).

Thus, from Genesis to Revelation, the Bible is as dogmatic as dogmatic can be concerning origins: "All things were made through Him, and without Him nothing was made that was made" (John 1:2, NKJV).

And that's because origins matter, even greatly. Nothing we believe as Adventists, even as Christians, makes sense apart from origins. What does Christ's death mean apart from His being the one whom the Father "hath appointed heir of all things, by whom also he made the worlds" (Hebrews 1:2)? What is redemption if God didn't create our world? What can we possibly be redeemed from in an atheistic universe? Without God as Creator, what is salvation? From what, and for what, are we saved? How can one understand the Fall except in the context of Creation? From where have we fallen, and to what are we to be restored? Apart from the biblical account of origins, what is the Second Coming except a fable, like Prometheus bringing fire to the earth? What is grace, reconciliation, and justification if our origins are not in a God who, by virtue of His creatorship, bestows upon us grace, reconciliation, and justification? What do we need grace for? To whom are we reconciled? Why do we need to be justified?

Separated from the truth of Creation, the most basic Christian doctrines must be relegated to myths of no more authenticity than Orpheus's descent to the underworld or Batman's battles with Penguin in Gotham City. Little, if not nothing at all, that we believe as Christians, much less as Adventists, has validity apart from our understanding of our origins as laid out in the Bible. Creation, literally, is the foundation upon which everything rests that we believe as Christians—and with that foundation gone, the structure crumbles.

No wonder, then, that the first verse of the Bible isn't, "For God so loved the world, that he gave his only begotten Son, that whosoever believeth in him should not perish, but have everlasting life" (John 3:16) or "God commendeth his love toward us, in that, while we were yet sinners, Christ died for us" (Romans 5:8) or "Therefore being justified by faith, we have peace with God through our Lord Jesus Christ" (Romans 5:1). The Bible doesn't begin with a statement about Christology, soteriology, or eschatology; Scripture doesn't introduce itself by talking about God's love, the objective atonement, or the Second Coming because these truths, no matter how crucial, sacred, or fundamental, make no sense apart from the words "In the beginning, God created the heavens and the earth" (Genesis 1:1).

This is the bottom-line foundation upon which all that is human rests. It's turtles all the way down—until here. Everything we believe, either secular or sacred, is premised on something, and no matter how far back we go, no matter how acutely, sharply, and finely we pare down our premises, we can't go back further than Genesis 1:1. We can speculate on the birth of the universe, the Big Bang, or ask as Augustine did rhetorically, "What was God doing before he made the heavens and the earth?"[7] but concerning the essentials of human existence, the buck stops at "In the beginning." Any system of thought—moral, ontological, or teleological—that isn't based on this premise is, of existential necessity, wrong, no matter how internally coherent, logical, and rational. It all begins at Creation, and apart from that nothing really makes sense, which again is why Isaiah spends so much time on origins.

"To whom will you liken me, and to whom will I be equal?" says the Holy One. Lift up high your eyes, and see who has created these things, who has brought forth by number their host; He has called all of them by name; from the multitude of His strength and the might of His power not one fails. . . . I will put the cedar, the shittah tree, the myrtle and the oil tree in the wilderness; I will set the fir, the pine and the boxwood together in the desert. In order that they will see and know and consider and understand together that the hand of the Lord has done this, and the Holy One of Israel has created it. . . . Israel shall be saved in the Lord, an eternal salvation. You will not be ashamed nor humiliated forever and ever. For thus says the Lord, the Creator of the heavens; He is the God who formed the earth. He made it; He established it; not in vain He created it. To be inhabited He formed it. "I am the Lord and there is no other" (Isaiah 40:25, 26; 41:19, 20; 45:17, 18).

Isaiah's words, if always relevant, are especially interesting in light of recent developments in the scientific world. Though not given much play in the secular press, modern science has been experiencing a radical change in its most fundamental assertions about the nature of the universe. At the heart of this "quiet revolution" is "the Anthropic Principle" (from the Greek word for "man," *anthropos*), which openly defies many of the modern, common "isms"—Marxism, secularism, existentialism, post-modernism, humanism, naturalism, positivism—all of which are premised on the common belief that we're here from blind chance alone, nothing but "an accidental collation of atoms" that has left us as the unfortunate byproducts of a random, even unfriendly, universe.

"The ancient covenant is in pieces," wrote biologist Jacques Monod, "man at last knows that he is alone in the unfeeling immensity of the universe, out of which he has emerged only by chance. Neither his destiny nor his duty have been written down."[8]

That's one way to look at it, though the Anthropic Principle says that rather than us being here "only by chance," man is the *ultimate end and purpose of the whole universe*—a position that goes even much farther than what biblical creationists believe! According to this principle, "far from being some curious sideshow or accident, humanity, or life at least, appear to be the goal toward which the entire universe has been intricately orchestrated, the logical center around which a whole host of physical values and relations had been exquisitely and precisely arranged."[9]

The gist of the Anthropic Principle is this: The universe is so finely and sensitively tuned, so delicate in its balance, that if any one of a number of crucial variables were off even by the slightest, almost infinitesimal, percentage, then humanity could not exist. The conclusion that many scientists are reaching from this evidence is that the whole universe appears to have been made with man (*anthropos*) in mind.

Paul Davies, professor of mathematical physics at the University of Adelaide (and who is not a biblical creationist) gives an example of why scientists are moving away from the notion of a random universe. Talking about the balance between gravity (which pulls objects toward each other) and the force of the Big Bang (which pushes objects away from each other), Davies wrote, "Had the Big Bang been weaker, the cosmos would have soon fallen back on itself in a big crunch. On the other hand, had it been stronger, the cosmic material would have dispersed so rapidly that galaxies would not have formed. Either way the structure of the universe seems to depend very sensitively on the precise matching of explosive rigor to gravitating power."[10]

How precisely? Davies writes that if the force of the Big Bang had been off only as much as one part in a staggering $10^{60}$, we wouldn't be here. "To give some meaning to these numbers," Davies continues, "suppose you wanted to fire a bullet at a one-inch target on the other side of the observable universe, twenty billion light years away. Your aim would have to be accurate to that same part in $10^{60}$."[11]

Donald Page of Princeton University's Institute for Advanced Study (who is not a biblical creationist either) has written that the odds of human life existing have been placed at one to $10,000,000,000^{124}$—a mind boggling number when you realize that the number of seconds (yes, *seconds!*) the universe is believed to have existed is only $10^{18}$ or that the number of subatomic particles (gluons, mesons, muons, pions, leptons, hadrons, the real small stuff) in the whole universe is $10^{80}$.[12]

No wonder Paul Davies wrote: "I cannot believe that our existence in this universe is a mere quirk of fate, an accident of history, an incidental blip in the great cosmic drama. Our involvement is too intimate. The physical species *Homo* may count for nothing, but the existence of mind in some organism on some planet in the universe is surely a fact of fundamental significance. Through conscious beings the universe has generated self-awareness. This can be no trivial detail, no minor byproduct of mindless, purposeless forces. We are truly meant to be here."[13]

Of course we are, which is why the Lord through Isaiah says: "I have made the earth, and I, even I, have created man upon it. My hands stretched forth the heavens, and all their host I have commanded. . . . For thus says the Lord, the Creator of the heavens; He is the God who formed the earth. He made it; He established it; not in vain He created it" (Isaiah 45:12, 18).

Origins matter, even greatly, which is why the Bible, especially Isaiah, spends so much time dealing with them. And what our origins tell us is that we have so many reasons to exult in the hope, in the promises, in the ultimate destiny that our Creator has guaranteed for us. Origins matter, not just because they tell us where we came from, or even why we're here or how we should act, but most importantly, they tell us where we're ultimately going and what's in store when we arrive: "For, behold, I create new heavens and a new earth: and the former shall not be remembered, nor come into mind" (Isaiah 65:17).

---

[1]Von Schelling, *Philosophical Letters on Dogmatism and Criticism*, quoted in Frederick Copleston, S. J., *History of Philosophy, vol. VII: Modern Philosophy—From the Post Kantian Idealists to Marx, Kirkegaard, and Nietzsche* (New York: Image Books, 1994), 100.

[2]Stephen Hawking, *A Brief History of Time* (New York: Bantam Books, 1988), 1.
[3]Houston Smith, *Beyond the Post-Modern Mind* (Wheaton, Ill.: Theosophical Publishing House, 1982), 52.
[4]"Wisdom" wrote Aristotle, "is knowledge about . . . causes and principles." *Metaphysics: The Complete Works of Aristotle,* Princeton/Bollingen Series LXXI, (Princeton, N. J.: Princeton University Press, 1991), 2:1553.
[5]Bertrand Russell, *Why I Am Not a Christian* (New York: Simon & Schuster, 1957), 106, 107.
[6]Ronald F. Youngblood, *The Book of Genesis* (Grand Rapids, Mich.: Baker Book House, 1991), 23. "As a special theological term," says the *Theological Dictionary of the Old Testament,* "*bara* is used to clearly express the incomparability of the creative work of God in contrast to all secondary products and likenesses made from already existing material by man."
[7]*Confessions,* 262.
[8]Jacques Monod, *Chance and Necessity* (London: Collins Press, 1972), 176.
[9]Patrick Glynn, "Beyond the Death of God," *National Review,* May 6, 1996, 30.
[10]Paul Davies, *God & the New Physics* (New York: Simon & Schuster, 1983), 197.
[11]Interestingly enough, the word *tohu,* translated "vain" in the last verse, comes also from the Genesis creation account: "And the earth was without form (*tohu*) and void" (Genesis 1:2). *Tohu,* although appearing nineteen times in various contexts throughout the Hebrew Bible, is used far more by Isaiah (eleven times) than by any other biblical author—more evidence of how important the creation theme is in the book.
[12]Dietrick E. Thomsen, "The Quantum Universe: A Zero-Point Fluctuation?" *Science News,* August 3, 1985, 125.
[13]Paul Davies, *The Mind of God* (New York: Simon & Schuster, 1992), 232.

# Repairers of the Breach

*"Earth and heaven also proclaim that they did not create themselves. 'We exist,' they tell us, 'because we were made. And this is proof that we did not make ourselves. For to make ourselves we should have had to exist before our existence began.' "*
*—St. Augustine[1]*

With creation so heavily emphasized in Isaiah, it's no surprise that the Sabbath—God's eternal, indestructible, and immutable sign of His creative power—is emphasized in Isaiah's book as well.

Thus says the Lord, "Keep judgment, and do righteousness, for my salvation is near to come, and my righteousness to be revealed. Blessed is the man who will do this, and the son of man who seizes hold of it: who keeps the Sabbath from polluting it, and keeps his hand from doing any evil. Let not the son of the stranger who has joined himself to the Lord say, uttering, 'The Lord has utterly separated me from his people;' let not the eunuch say, 'Behold, I am a dry tree.' " For thus says the Lord to the eunuchs who keep my Sabbaths, and choose that in which I delight and who are taking hold of my covenant: "I give to them in my house and my wall a place and a name better than that of sons and daughters; an everlasting name I will give to them that shall not be cut off. And the sons of the strangers who join themselves to the Lord, to serve Him, and to love the name of the Lord, to be His servants, all who keep the Sabbath from polluting it and those who take hold of my covenant—even them I will bring to my holy mountain and make them rejoice in my house of prayer. Their burnt offerings and their sacrifices will be acceptable upon my altar, for my house will be called a house of prayer for all people" (Isaiah 56:1-7).

The Lord God will guide you continually, and He will satisfy your soul in drought and make strong your bones. And you will be like a watered garden, and like a spring of water whose waters don't fail. And those from you will build the ancient waste place: you will raise up the foundations of many generations, and you will be called The Repairers of the Breach, restorers of the paths to dwell in. "If you turn away your foot from the Sabbath, from doing your delight in my holy day, and call the Sabbath a delight, the holy of the Lord, and honorable, and if you will honor it, not doing your ways, and finding your pleasures and speaking your words, then you will delight yourself in the Lord and I will make you ride upon the high places of the earth, and He will feed you with the inheritance of your father, Jacob, for the mouth of the Lord has spoken it" (Isaiah 58:11-14).

These verses radiate, not only beautiful imagery but powerful, "present-truth" theology as well. They echo, first, a key theme that reverberates through Isaiah's quill: that a saving relationship with God wasn't limited to the Hebrew nation alone, but that righteousness, salvation, and eternal life were to be given also to the Gentiles. Isaiah prefigures, by centuries, the spread of the gospel to all nations. "And the Gentiles shall come to your light, and kings to the

brightness of your rising" (Isaiah 60:3). "And the Gentiles will see
your righteousness, and all kings your glory, and you will be called
by a new name, which the mouth of the Lord will specify" (Isaiah
62:2). "And this gospel of the kingdom shall be preached in all the
world for a witness unto all nations; and then shall the end come"
(Matthew 24:14).

But these verses also teach that because salvation is for everyone, the Sabbath is, too, because both the Sabbath and salvation are
intricately entwined (another reason why the theme of salvation is so
prevalent in Isaiah, who isn't called "the gospel prophet" for nothing).

The Jews, in fact, have always viewed the Sabbath as a precursor,
a symbol, of Messianic redemption. According to the Talmud, if the
Jews "were to keep two Sabbaths according to their prescribed law,
they would immediately be redeemed."[2] Rabbi Walter S. Wurzburger
of Yeshiva University wrote: "Because of the close association between the Sabbath and the redemption, the liturgy for welcoming the
Sabbath includes a number of psalms that give vent to the feelings of
exhilaration and jubilation that will be precipitated by the establishment of the kingdom of God."[3] Or, as Abraham Joshua Heschel expressed it: "The Sabbath is an example of the world to come."[4] Christian author John McKenzie sees the link as well: "The coming of
salvation is associated with the observance of the Sabbath."[5]

No wonder Isaiah not only ties redemption to the Gentiles but the
Sabbath as well. Even these non-Jews, the "sons of the strangers"
who join themselves to the Lord, have the promise of redemption and
thus can enjoy the Sabbath, a symbol of that redemption. Almost
2,800 years before the Adventist Church, Isaiah expressed a central
component of our message, which is that the Sabbath is a universal
verity, a day for all the redeemed of every land. Here, in the *Old*
Testament (as opposed to the New, where the Sabbath was supposedly superseded by Sunday), Isaiah dispels the common misconcep-
tion that the Sabbath is binding only on Jews.[6, 7]

The Sabbath has always been "present truth" (even if, according to our understanding of Revelation, it will become a *more pressing* truth as we approach the end time), if for no other reason than because all human beings—Jews, Gentiles, eunuchs—for all of history have existed only because God created them and because the Sabbath, from Eden, remains the sign of that creation as well as a symbol of redemption for the redeemed. The Sabbath is present truth in every age. If it were possible to find a group of people who were not in Adam's loins, who don't owe their existence to God's creative power, then perhaps one could argue that the Sabbath isn't for them, and therefore it is not universal. But because it's not likely to find any such group, the Sabbath remains present truth all the time for everyone because everyone always owes his or her existence to God.

Ellen White, meanwhile, ties these specific Sabbath verses in Isaiah to our calling today, as a church:

> As the end approaches, the testimonies of God's servants will become more decided and more powerful, flashing the light of truth upon the systems of error and oppression that have so long held the supremacy. The Lord has sent us messages for this time, that will establish Christianity upon an eternal basis; and all who believe the present truth, must stand, not in their own wisdom, but in God's wisdom, and raise up the foundations of many generations; and they will be registered in the books of heaven as "repairers of the breach," the "restorer of paths to dwell in."[8]

And, no doubt, paths do need restoration, and breaches need repair. And the Sabbath truth can do it—a reality recently hammered home when Willow Creek Community Church in Chicago staged a public debate between a Christian and an atheist on the evidence for the existence of God. The poor atheist was intellectually, verbally, and logically outgunned by the brilliant eloquence of Dr. Craig. Nevertheless—while neither denying or affirming evolution—Dr. Craig did say that he saw no conflict between his religion and evolutionary theory. He asserted that God could have used evolution in the creation process. He suggested that "we'll just have to wait and see what the evidence is"—that is, whether it's pro or con the evolutionary scheme—but that he could accept either conclusion. The only time the atheist scored was at this point, when he argued (correctly) that evolution was how Satan would create the world, not God.

Craig's position symbolizes how much the old paths need restoration and the breaches need repair. How could Craig, a brilliant, well-educated Christian, allow himself to assert that there is harmony between biblical Christianity and the standard evolutionary model, which teaches that all species arose from a common, simple life form after millions of years of a brutal process in which only the strongest survive? That indeed sounds more like Satan's methods than God's. Though, no doubt, the answer is complicated, one facet of the explanation is easy: William Lane Craig, like a majority of professing Christians, does not keep the seventh-day Sabbath—and thus, like the majority of Christians, Dr. Craig is severed from the one thing that, more than anything else, could save him from something so totally anti-biblical, anti-Christian, and wrong as evolution.

He's not alone either. The evolutionary *zeitgeist* has so blinded Christian culture that millions can't see the blatant contradiction between Christianity and classical evolution. Pope John Paul II, in an address to the Pontifical Academy of Sciences, all but endorsed evolution a few years ago. The pope, echoing the encyclical *Humani Generis* (1950) written by Pius XII (which asserted that no opposition existed between evolution and Christianity) said that "new knowledge leads to the recognition of the theory of evolution as more than a hypothesis."[9]

Even such an unapologetically conservative journal as *First Things* published an article called "Untangling Evolution," in which the author argued for a view of origins that mixes a rapid materialistic evolution with Christianity. "The mutations that led from the first single-celled creature to the genus Homo," wrote Stephen Barr, "may have been chance events from a certain point of view, but as Pope John Paul II has said, every one of them was foreseen and willed by God."[10]

Whose God? Certainly not the one depicted in Genesis.

When asked in 1874, "What is Darwinism?" Presbyterian theologian Charles Hodge answered, "It is atheism." He was right, because that's all evolution ever was or ever will be—an attempt to understand our existence apart from the concept of a Creator God who purposely put us here. Why can't most Christians see that evolution—based on scientific naturalism which insists that the cosmos is a closed system of purely material cause-and-effect relationships that can never be influenced by anything outside of materialist nature (such as the God who said "Let there be light")—is incompatible with Christianity? One reason, for sure, is that these people don't keep the biblical Sabbath, and this has left them wide open to something as bogus as evolution, because at its core evolution utterly negates all that the Sabbath stands for. (Of course, nonSabbath-keeping Christians exist who accept the literal account of Creation in Genesis as Adventists do, but they're an infinitesimally small percentage of Christianity).

What's interesting about the pope's statement, as well as the readiness with which Christians have swallowed current trends (clothed in the stately and authoritative garb of science) is that evolution has never had universal acceptance in the scientific community (Darwin's biggest critics at first weren't clerics but fossil experts). In recent years Darwin's theories have been under attack within and without the scientific community. Coming from different perspectives, experts are asking questions about data that undermine the most fundamental assumptions of classical evolutionary theory. "It is ironic," wrote John Woodridge, "that some evangelical scholars are discounting Bible statements about nature and history at the very time evolutionary thought is in such flux."[11]

One of the most devastating attacks against evolution has been hurled by Berkeley law professor Philip E. Johnson. After years of using his critical skills as a lawyer to investigate the claims of evolution, Johnson shows in his book, *Darwin on Trial,* that the standard, textbook model of Darwinian, naturalistic, biological evolution— which generations have been taught with a dogmatic fervor comparable to left-wing Adventism—is based on evidence that varies from weak to nonexistent. Point by point, he looks at the common claims— natural selection, the fossil record, mutations, the pre-Cambrian explosion, molecular biology—and argues that, when closely investigated, these not only don't fit the evolutionary scheme (the way we have been assured they do) but actually work against it.[12]

Besides Johnson's book, one of the greatest of the recent popular assaults on the Darwinian fallacy has been from biochemistry professor Michael Behe, whose powerful arguments in his *Darwin's Black Box* have forced evolutionists and the media to confront them (their usual tactic is to dismiss criticism as "unscientific babble" and make *ad hominum* attacks by calling critics "creationists"). Behe, a kind of Laodicean Catholic, stresses "I am not a creationist,"[13] in the sense of believing in a young-earth, literal, six-day creation as taught in Genesis. In a *New York Times* editorial (the fact that he was asked to contribute to the *New York Times* shows how seriously he has been taken) he even wrote that he has "no quarrel with the idea of a common descent,"[14] a position basic to evolutionary theory. Nevertheless in the same editorial, he sums up his challenge to the theory in this way: "[T]he complex design of a cell has provoked me to stake out a distinctly minority view on the question of what caused evolution. I believe that Darwin's mechanism for evolution doesn't explain much of what we see under a microscope. Cells are simply too complex to have evolved randomly; intelligence was required to produce them."[15]

The gist of his book (a heavier read than Phillip Johnson's), and Behe's dagger in Darwin's heart, is what Behe calls "irreducible complexity," the idea that cells are so constructed that if any one of a number of components (or functions) were missing, the cell could not possibly work. Hence the notion that these somehow "evolved," that each part, or function, slowly and gradually grew into its specific role is not scientifically tenable.

> By irreducibly complex I mean a single system, composed of several well-matched, interacting parts that contribute to the basic function, wherein the removal of any one of the parts causes the system to effectively cease functioning. An irreducibly complex system cannot be produced directly (that is, by continuously improving the initial function, which continues to work by the same mechanism) by slight, successive modifications of a precursor system, because any precursor to an irreducibly complex system that is missing a part is by definition nonfunctional. An irreducibly complex biological system, if there is such a thing, would be a powerful challenge to Darwinian evolution. Since natural selection can only choose systems that are already working, then if a biological system cannot be produced gradually it would have to arise as an integrated unit, in one fell swoop, for natural selection to have anything to act on.[16]

Behe then carefully shows that numerous irreducibly complex systems do exist within the human body, which means that according to his definition, they could not have evolved in an incremental, step-by-step manner as evolution presupposes. Behe describes some irreducibly complex systems—everything from blood clotting to vision to the immune system to vesicular transport to the biosynthesis of AMP.[17] Behe concludes that these irreducibly complex biological processes could have arisen only from "intelligent design," a concept that Isaiah paralleled thousands of years ago with these words about the Intelligent Designer:

> Who has measured the waters in the hollow of his hand, or

balanced the heavens with a span, or calculated the dust of the earth in a scale, or weighed the mountains in a scale or the hills in a balance? Who has directed the Spirit of the Lord, or who has taught Him? With whom did He take counsel, who made Him wise or taught Him the path of judgment, or taught Him knowledge, or made Him know the way of understanding? (Isaiah 40:12-14).

Behe has expressed another interesting, and crucial, idea—that the "most powerful reason for science's reluctance to embrace a theory of intelligent design is also based on a philosophical consideration. Most people, including many important and well-respected scientists, just don't *want* there to be anything beyond nature. They don't want a supernatural being to affect nature, no matter how brief or constructive the interaction may have been. In other words, like young-earth creationists, they bring an a priori philosophical commitment to their science that restricts what kinds of explanations they will accept about the physical world."[18]

No one, especially Christians, who—despite an unrelenting onslaught of "scientific" assumptions to the contrary—accept the Genesis creation account as it reads, should miss Behe's point. Though, at least in the earlier years of the seventeenth and eighteenth centuries, science and religion were not necessarily at odds (of course, exceptions existed, such as the church's refusal to look through Galileo's telescope), over time science became exclusively materialistic and naturalistic, dogmatically exorcizing any supernatural or theological considerations from its domain. If science and theology agreed, fine (so much the better for theology); if not, then science—supposedly based on unfiltered, objective, rational, and systematic facts—would prevail over something as nebulous, subjective, and arbitrary as religion. (Again, the fundamental question is, Who is the final authority?) The only alternative for religion, it seemed, in an age when science had become almost the sole arbiter of truth, was to tweak, compromise, and bowdlerize its beliefs in order to make them fit prevailing scientific notions, no matter how blatantly opposed those notions were to basic religious truth. And nothing better exemplifies Christian kowtowing to popular trends (especially when authoritatively garbed under the label of "science") than its almost universal acquiescence to evolution.[19]

In his classic work, *A History of Science*, Sir William Cecil Dampier wrote: "Science, we have now come to understand, cannot deal with ultimate reality; it can only draw a picture of nature as seen by the human mind. Our ideas are in a sense real in that ideal picture world, but the individual things represented are pictures and not realities."[20]

Even science can give only idealized pictures of reality, not reality itself. After all, what science can teach us the most overwhelming reality in the world—the fact that Christ died for our sins and that "in him we live, move and have our being" (Acts 17:28)? Absolutely nothing, only the Bible can, which is why Satan has worked so hard to use evolution to destroy faith in the Bible and the God of the Bible. Yet despite the almost pandemic pervasiveness of evolution (much like the Ptolemaic concept of an earth-centered universe that dominated its day), the Sabbath is an impenetrable, indestructible bulwark against an onslaught that has decimated the ranks of Christians, separating them from the foundation upon which rest all the truths they profess to believe. Thus Isaiah, in proclaiming the Sabbath so forcefully, presents a radical, in-your-face rejection of the evolutionary hypothesis and all philosophical, teleological, and moral ramifications that the theory carries of necessity.

Isaiah contains a powerful recapitulation and magnification of the Genesis creation account. Isaiah takes those truths, frames them in different language, puts them in a different context, in a different manner, and with robust eloquence proclaims them down through the centuries, even to our time. And what the prophet says to us is that we should not be afraid to stand almost alone (as we do) with our literal interpretation of the Genesis creation. What Isaiah says is that we must be "repairers of the breach," because the crack is not only wide and deep but foundational and goes to the heart of what it means to be a Christian. Isaiah proclaims that the Sabbath message (and all that it contains) is a truth that the world (and all that it lacks) needs. Isaiah says that we must never capitulate before "science," for science is only man's interpretation of how things appear. Science has been wrong before, and nothing guarantees it can't be wrong again (its almost universal acceptance of the evolutionary theory, in fact, proves it's wrong now).

Isaiah, essentially, reaffirms our interpretation of the world, one that comes not from the creature but from the Creator. Isaiah says, Don't believe in origins according to Charles Darwin or Stephen Jay Gould; believe in origins according to the Originator Himself, the One "who has made all things, stretching out the heavens, spreading out the earth" (Isaiah 44:24).

"Take heed to yourselves, that your heart be not deceived, and ye turn aside, and serve other gods, and worship them," reads Deuteronomy 11:16 (KJV). In this text, the word *deceived* literally means "open." It could read, "Take heed to yourselves, that your heart be not *opened*, and ye turn aside. . . ."

Isaiah tells us that we don't need to be open to lies, open to false gods, open to erroneous concepts of who we are, how we got here, why we're here, and where we're ultimately going. Isaiah, instead, points us backward, to the beginning, to our origins, for in them is the foundation upon which rests not only truth—but the hope, the promise, and the great and glorious future that this truth unfolds before us with a certainty and surety as certain and sure as God Himself.

---

[1] St. Augustine, *Confessions* R. S. Pine-Coffin, trans. (New York: Penguin Books, 1961), 256.
[2] Tractate Shab, 118b.
[3] Walter S. Wurnberge, "A Jewish Theology and Philosophy of the Sabbath," in *The Sabbath in Jewish and Christian Traditions,* Tamara C. Eskenazi, Daniel J. Harrington, S. J., and William H. Shea, eds. (New York: Crossroad, 1991), 145.
[4] Abraham Joshua Heschel, *The Sabbath* (New York: Farrar, Straus, and Giroux, 1983), 73.

[5]John L. McKenzie, *Second Isaiah*, Anchor Bible Series (New York: Doubleday & Co., 1967), 150.

[6]Baptist preacher Walter Chantry, in a book urging Sunday observance, wrote that "anyone who claims that the Sabbath is uniquely Jewish is arguing against Moses, the founding prophet of Judaism. He is also plainly contradicting the express teaching of our Lord Jesus Christ. It is simply not a defensible position. It is not the Bible's position in either the Old Testament or the New. . . . The Sabbath is an issue of morality which touches all mankind from the time of creation." Walter Chantry, *Call the Sabbath a Delight* (Carlisle, Penn.: The Banner of Truth Trust, 1991), 56.

[7]Jewish philosopher Martin Buber wrote that because the Sabbath is rooted in something as universal as creation (after all, even Gentiles owe their existence to God), "the Sabbath is common property of all, and all ought to enjoy its benefits without restriction." Martin Buber, *Moses* (New York: Oxford University Press, 1946), 84.

[8]*Adventist Review*, December 13, 1992.

[9]Quoted in *First Things*, March 28, 1997, 28. Though debate exists over exactly what the pope meant (Cal Thomas wrote "it's clear that the pope was not watering down or liberalizing the church's view that the origins of man remained open to debate"), and though the secular press made hay with his address (according to the *New York Times*, the pope now "has put the teaching authority of the Roman Catholic church firmly behind the view that the human body may not have been the immediate creation of God"), John Paul's words exemplify just how much evolution has polluted the Christian psyche.

[10]Stephen Barr, "Untangling Evolution," *First Things*, December 1997, 17.

[11]John Woodridge, "Does the Bible Teach Science?" *Bibliotheca Sacra* 142, July/September, 1985, 205.

[12]For instance, according to Johnson, the fossil record, supposedly the foundation of the evolutionary model, far from proving the theory, seems to disprove it instead. First, the transitional forms, from one species to another, don't exist in the fossil record as they are supposed to (the gaps are still here, even more than a century after Darwin acknowledged them as a problem). Second, the fossil record shows that species, for the most part, remain static. Third, the fossil record shows what is known as the pre-Cambrian explosion, in "which all the animal phyla appear in the rocks of this period without a trace of the evolutionary ancestors that Darwinists require."

Johnson then refers to the "punctuated equilibrium" theory of paleontologist Stephen Jay Gould, which teaches (contrary to Darwin) that evolutionary changes, instead of coming gradually, happened in spurts (this is Gould's attempt to deal with the lack of evidence for the gradual transitional phases basic to evolutionary theory). Johnson even quotes Gould as admitting that "the history of most fossil species includes two features particularly inconsistent with gradualism [standard evolution] . . . (1) Stasis. Most species exhibit no direction change during their tenure on earth. They appear in the fossil record looking pretty much the same as when they disappear. . . . (2) Sudden appearance. In any local area, a species does not arise gradually by the steady transformation of its ancestors; it appears all at once and 'fully formed.' "

No wonder Johnson, who isn't a biblical creationist, writes, "In short, if evolution means the gradual change of one kind of organism into another, the outstanding characteristic of the fossil record is the absence of evidence for evolution."

[13]Quoted in "Meeting Darwin's Wager," *Christianity Today,* April 28, 1997, 18.

[14]Michael Behe, "Darwin Under the Microscope," *New York Times*, October 29, 1996, A25.

[15]*Ibid.*

[16]Michael Behe, *Darwin's Black Box* (New York: The Free Press, 1996), 39.

[17]*Ibid.,* 151. More than a century earlier, Darwin admitted: "If it could be demonstrated that any complex organ existed, which could not possibly have been formed by numerous successive, slight modifications, then my theory would absolutely break down." What Behe demonstrates is that these irreducibly complex systems "could not have possible been formed by numerous, successive, slight modifications."

What's fascinating, and key to Behe's argument, is that almost *no* papers in scientific journals ever explain how these fantastically complex processes could be produced by the evolutionary process.

"No one at Harvard University," he writes, "no one at the National Institutes of Health, no member of the National Academy of Sciences, no Nobel Prize winner—no one at all can give a detailed account of how the cilium, or vision, or blood clotting, or any complex biochemical process might have developed in a Darwinian fashion."

Behe continues: "The problem for Darwinian evolution is this: if only the end product of a complicated biosynthetic path is used in the cell, how did the pathway evolve in steps? If A, B, and C have no use other than as precursors to D, what advantage is there to an organism to make just A? Or, if it makes A to make B? If a cell needs AMP, what good will it do to just make Intermediate III, or IV, or V? On their face, metabolic pathways where intermediates are not useful present severe challenges to a Darwinian scheme of evolution."

[18]*Ibid.,* 243.

[19]What's even more sad about Christians being bullied in this compromise—in blatant disregard for the teaching of Genesis, of Isaiah, indeed, of all Scripture—is that science can, in many ways, be as subjective as faith. Many people don't realize that science, like faith, has its own unprovable assumptions. Scientists, based on their own "a priori philosophical commitment," automatically exclude certain notions from their thinking. For example, as Behe wrote, they "don't want a supernatural being to affect nature"—and this subjective bias clearly restricts the direction of their scientific endeavors.

One of the most influential texts in the twentieth century, Thomas Kuhn's *The Structure of Scientific Revolutions,* dealt with the subjectivity of science. Showing how scientists, working with their own biased, majority concept of how the world is supposed to work (called a "paradigm"), Kuhn argued that instead of proceeding in an objective manner with one scientific breakthrough building linearly upon another one, scientists usually plan experiments, devise instruments, and interpret data solely through the lens of whatever subjective paradigm happens to be in vogue. This is "normal science," which is nothing but "an attempt to force nature into the preformed and relatively inflexible box that the paradigm supplies." Any phenomena, he wrote, that don't "fit in the box are often not seen at all. Nor do scientists aim to invent new theories, and they are often intolerant of those invented by others."

According to Kuhn, only when an accumulation of conflicting data formed a "crisis" did the old paradigm give away to another one, just as subjective as the previous paradigm. He called this shift a "scientific revolution," which he compares to a political one.

[20]W. C. Dampier, *A History of Science* (Cambridge: Cambridge University Press, 1966), 35.

# Beings and Nothingness

*"The essence of man is his freedom.*
*Sin is committed in that freedom."*
*—Reinhold Niebuhr*[1]

Have you ever thought about how many crucial, substantive, and basic components of your life are beyond your control?

From your birth (an event forced upon you without your choice, input, or acquiescence) to your genes, to your early environment, and up through the whole history of the world prior to your existence—your life has been affected by forces over which you have no say or influence.

Also, if an omnipotent God who knows the beginning from the end knew a thousand years ago that at this instant you'd be reading *these words in italics*, did you have any other choice but to read them? "Whatever anyone ever does," wrote Gilbert Ryle, "whatever happens anywhere to anything, could not *not* be done or happen, if it was true beforehand [or if God already knew beforehand] that it was going to be done or going to happen."[2] Isaiah, Daniel, and David detailed the death of Christ centuries before the event, which proves, no doubt, that the Lord already knew what Judas, Caiaphas, Herod, and Pilate would do centuries be-

fore they did it. Did Judas, Caiaphas, Herod, and Pilate therefore
have no choice in their actions?

It's no wonder that much intellectual thought has taken the uncomfortable position against free will. "Modern philosophy," wrote
Sir James Jean, "also seems to have come to the conclusion that there
is no real alternative to determinism, which the result that the question now discussed is no longer whether we are free but why we think
we are free."[3]

However, philosophical speculation regarding the issue of free
will aside—what does one do with the first few verses of Isaiah 55?

> Ho, all who thirst, come to the water, and who doesn't have
> silver—come, buy, and eat; come, buy wine and milk but not
> with silver and not with cost. Why do you spend silver for what
> isn't bread, and why do you toil for what cannot satisfy? Listen,
> listen to me, and eat well and pamper yourself in fatness. Incline
> your ear and come to me, and your soul will live and I will cut
> with you an everlasting covenant, the faithful loving kindness
> of David (Isaiah 55:1-3).

Most of the verbs in these verses—"come," "buy," "eat," "listen,"
"incline"—are imperatives, expressing a command or a plea. In other
words, in the Bible when God speaks to man in the imperative, as He
often does, what can that mean other than that we have free will, at
least regarding the things of God?

All through Isaiah the Lord uses verbs in forms that make no
sense apart from human freedom—especially in context. Note these
verses (the imperative verbs have been italicized in each one):

"*Listen* to me, you who pursue righteousness, who seek the Lord;
*look* to the rock from where you were hewn, and the hole of the pit
from where you were dug" (Isaiah 51:1). "Thus says the Lord, *keep*
judgment and *do* justice" (Isaiah 56:1). "*Come,* and let us reason
together, says the Lord" (Isaiah 1:15). Why would the Lord so

earnestly beckon if His people had no choice but to obey, or were predetermined before birth to obedience?

*"Turn* to me and be saved, all you ends of the earth, for I am the Lord and there is no other" (Isaiah 45:22). *"Hear* the Word of the Lord, rulers of Sodom; *listen* to the law of our God, people of Gomorrah" (Isaiah 1:10). What can these verses mean if man's actions have been predetermined? And if they are predetermined, did God choose beforehand to make some people disobedient? And if He did, why does He bother to call them to Himself?

Though the verbs in the next few verses aren't in the imperative, these verses also teach the inescapable reality of moral freedom: "I am sought by those who didn't ask, and I am found by those who didn't seek me. I said, 'Here I am, here I am,' to a nation that did not call my name. I have spread out my hands all day to a stubborn people who walk in a way not good, after their own thoughts" (Isaiah 65:1, 2). "They have chosen their ways, and their soul delights in their abominations" (Isaiah 66:3). "Then I will number you to the sword, and all of you will bow down to the slaughter, because I called but you did not answer, I spoke but you did not hear. But you did evil in my eyes and what I delighted in you did not choose" (Isaiah 65:12).

Not only Isaiah but the entire Word of God testifies to human freedom. From Eden to the Apocalypse, the Bible writers in one venue or another, either through narrative, poetry, or theological discourse, reveal the reality of free will. Little, or no, Bible truth makes any sense apart from human freedom.

For example, "sin" is a nonsensical notion apart from moral autonomy. Even hard-nosed atheist Bertrand Russell understood that "the conception of 'sin' is closely connected with the belief in free will, for, if our actions are determined by causes over which we have no control, retributive punishment can have no justification."[4] How could there be a final reckoning if we didn't have moral freedom? (The concept of morality itself doesn't make sense apart from free-dom. Can something even be "moral" if it has no choice in its actions?) If we do not have free will, Albert Einstein once asked, "how is it possible to think of holding men responsible for their deeds and thoughts before such an almighty Being? In giving out punishments and rewards he would be . . . passing judgment on himself."[5]

Yet Scripture is unequivocal about judgment ("For God shall bring all deeds to judgment, with every secret thing whether good or evil" [Ecclesiastes 12:14]), about punishment ("And I will punish the world for its evil, and the wicked for their iniquity" [Isaiah 13:11]), and about reward ("Rejoice ye in that day, and leap for joy: for, behold, your reward is great in heaven" [Luke 6:23]). How could these things be, unless we can make choices that merit reward or punishment? The truth, of course, is that we can make those choices; we always do.

Therefore, no matter how many factors that affect our lives exist beyond our reach—such as the twists and turns of our DNA or whether or not mother breast fed us or the burning of the Reichstag—the most crucial factor of our personal existence, the one that matters beyond any other and that can in fact help mitigate the impact of every other, is one that we *can* control—our relationship to God. The Lord is constantly seeking, through the power of His Holy Spirit, to bring us to a saving relationship with Him. How we respond is, ultimately, up to us; it's a matter of free choice. This is the eternal option, and it leaves all other options in the dust, because it's the one that determines not only how we live now but in the long run it determines the final rewards or punishment that inevitably come. You might not be able to choose your genes, your parents, or the weather, but you can choose to love and obey the Lord, who is seeking to save you from the mire of sin, death, and destruction that, among other things, your genes, parents, or the weather have left you in.

"The Lord is not slack concerning his promise, as some men count slackness; but is longsuffering to usward, not willing that any should perish, but that all should come to repentance" (2 Peter 3:9).

"Look unto me, and be ye saved, all the ends of the earth" (Isaiah 45:22).

"For this is good and acceptable in the sight of God our Saviour; who will have all men to be saved, and to come unto the knowledge of the truth. For there is one God, and one mediator between God and men, the man Christ Jesus; who gave himself a ransom for all, to be testified in due time" (1 Timothy 2:3-6).

In fact, Christ's death is something else that is beyond our control—like our grandparents, or Caesar's crossing the Rubicon. Apart from us, separate from us, without our choice, input, or influence—Jesus died on the cross, where He took upon Himself God's wrath for our sin. You can't change that fact any more than you can change the weather. All you can do is to choose your response by using free will.

Thus, however much our first birth and all the variables around it were beyond our control, our second birth, the new birth, isn't. That's *our* choice, and through it—whatever our circumstances—the Lord gives us a chance to start over. We have a new life, a new history, a new status before God, who wipes the slate clean with the blood of Jesus. "Therefore if any man be in Christ, he is a new creature: old things are passed away; behold, all things are become new" (2 Corinthians 5:17).

However indifferent, heartless, and uncaring the universe can seem, we can know by faith that far from being ignominiously dumped into a world controlled by cold, amoral, lifeless forces, we were created for a purpose by a loving God who is working everything out in such a manner that in the end all the rational beings in heaven and earth and beyond will freely shout "just and true are thy ways, thou King of saints" (Revelation 15:3). No matter how fatalistic or statistical or random events might seem, we can know that behind the façade of reality as it appears to our feeble sin-darkened minds, God is ultimately in control and will bring everything to the happiest ending possible. No matter how brutishly things beyond your power have been to you, an all-powerful, all-loving, caring God—One greater than any earthly and evanescent variable—will give comfort, healing, and power to cope for all who choose Him.

Yet so often He isn't chosen.

"Ho, all who thirst, come to the water, and who doesn't have silver—come, buy, and eat; come, buy wine and milk but not with silver and not with cost. *Why do you spend silver for what isn't bread, and why do you toil for what cannot satisfy?*" (Isaiah 55:1, 2, italics supplied).

Here, as through all Isaiah, as through *all the Bible* even, the Lord is calling people away from wasting their time, energy, and lives pursing what they think will make them happy, those things they think will answer their deepest needs and yet don't because they can't. They spend silver for what can't feed them and toil for what can't satisfy.

"Why does man feel so bad in the twentieth century?" wrote novelist Walker Percy. "Why does man feel so bad in the very age when, more than in any other age, he has succeeded in satisfying his needs and making over the world for his own use?"[6]

Because he hasn't satisfied his *real* needs, which is why he feels bad. He has toiled and spent silver for what isn't bread, when Isaiah promises that through the Lord you can "eat well and pamper yourself in fatness" (Isaiah 55:2).

The irony in these verses is that people toil (more literally, "weary themselves") and spend money in pursuit of what's ultimately empty, when the only thing that can satisfy takes no toil or money. God says to come, and He will feed us without silver and without cost because Christ, as Isaiah also teaches, paid the price Himself.

Isaiah is brimming with words that convey the emptiness, the void, the vanity, the nothingness and meaningless of so much of what people cling to, even as he calls them to reject those things for the only thing that could possibly fulfill their most insatiate longings.

"Behold you are *nothing*, and your work is of *nought*" (Isaiah 41:24, italics supplied). The word translated "nothing," *ayin*, is a particle of negation; the closest English equivalent is "not." *Ayin* is often translated "is not," "were not," "are not," "was not." For example,

"And Enoch walked with God, and *he was not,* for God took Him" (Genesis 5:24, italics supplied).

"No one calls for justice, nor judges in truth. They trust in *vanity* and speak *worthlessness*" (Isaiah 59:4, italics supplied). The word translated "vanity" is *tohu*, (also found in Genesis 1:2, "and the earth was *tohu* and void, and darkness was upon the face of the deep"). It means, essentially, "formlessness," "emptiness," "empty space," "unreality," "confusion." Meanwhile, the word for "worthlessness," *shav,* means "emptiness," "vanity," "nothingness."

"When you cry, let your assembled ones deliver you; but the wind shall carry them all away, and *vapor* shall take them" (Isaiah 57:13, italics supplied). The word *vapor* in this verse comes from *hbl,* which also means "vanity," "vainly," "to no purpose." As Solomon wrote "*Hbl* of *hbl*, all is *hbl*" (Ecclesiastes 1:12).

"And Egypt will help you in *vain* [*hbl*], to *no purpose*" (Isaiah 30:7, italics supplied). The phrase "no purpose" comes from a Hebrew word (*rik*) meaning "empty," "void," "idle," or "vainly."

"Behold, all of them are *nothing*; their works are *null*; *wind* and *empty* their molten images" (Isaiah 41:29, italics supplied). "Nothing" here is again *ayin*[7]; the word for "null" is *efs,* which expresses nonexistence, meaninglessness, or ceasing. "There is none [*efs*] besides me; I am the Lord and there is no [*ayin*] other" (Isaiah 45:6). "Wind" is *ruach*, commonly "breath," "wind," or "spirit." "Empty" is *tohu* again.

"For thus saith the Lord, you have sold yourselves for *nothing,* and you will be redeemed without money" (Isaiah 52:3, italics supplied). "Nothing" (*hinam*) means "for nought, or "without purpose" or "without cause."

"Woe to them who draw iniquity with cords of *vanity* [*shv*]" (Isaiah 5:18, italics supplied).

"All the nations are as *nothing* [*ayin*] before him; as *nothing* [*efs*] and void [*tohu*] they are deemed" (Isaiah 40:17, italics supplied).

"Those who make graven images; all of them are *vain* [*tohu*]"

(Isaiah 44:9, italics supplied).

Each of these words expresses the futility of the world and worldly ways. In contrast, Isaiah in all its depth, richness, and power, is ultimately a book about salvation, about the Second Coming, about the ensuing eternity that begins when Christ returns and makes the heavens and the earth over again. For this reason, the emptiness, the vanity, the nothingness of these words, used so profusely in Isaiah, becomes even more apparent in contrast to what God offers us both now and in eternity.

The last verse quoted—"Those who make graven images; all of them are *vain* [*tohu*]" (Isaiah 44:9, italics supplied)—comes from a chapter in Isaiah that symbolizes the futility, the vanity, and the ultimate emptiness of the wrong choices humans have so often made with their free wills, whether in the eighth century B.C. or the twentieth A.D.

Isaiah 44 begins with God's promise to fulfill the needs of His people. "For I will pour water upon the thirsty, and floods upon that which is dry; and I will pour out my Spirit upon your seed and my blessings upon your offspring" (verse 3).

The Lord then states again His supremacy, as He does through much of Isaiah. "Thus says the Lord, I am the King of Israel, his Redeemer, the Lord of Host. I am the first, and I am the last and besides me there is no [*ayin*] other God" (verse 6). In the next few verses the Lord emphasizes His power, His knowledge of the future, and His ability to control it, which is why He then says, "Do not fear, do not be afraid" (verse 8).

Isaiah then contrasts this affirmation of God's kingship, of His redemption, of His power, of His ability to satisfy the needs of His people with the emptiness and meaninglessness of idolatry. He writes about a man who hews down a tree to build a fire and then uses the rest of the wood to make an idol.

Then it [the wood] will be to the man for burning: he takes from it and warms himself; then he burns it and bakes bread;

then he makes a god and worships it. He makes a graven image and falls prostate before it. Part of it he burns with fire; with part he eats flesh; he then roasts meat and is filled. He is warm and says, "I am warm; I have seen the fire." And with the rest he makes a god, a graven image, and he falls prostrate before it and worships it, and he prays to it and says, "Save me, because you are my god" (verses 15-17).

Isaiah's point is the utter silliness, the futility of this false worship. This is the kind of man who "has shut his eyes from seeing" (verse 18). Even with the revelation of God, of His creative power and might, this man has chosen to go his own way, to worship his own gods, which either now, or in the end, cannot save. "He feeds on ashes; a deceived heart has turned him aside and will not deliver his soul, and he cannot say, 'Is there not a lie in my right hand?' " (verse 20). In other words, he's been so deceived by his wrong choices that he can't discern his error.

Of course, today, the details don't apply (most of us don't worship statues of wood), but the universal principle behind the details does apply, because everyone, in one way or another, worships. In today's secular society, men worship themselves, or their institutions, their heroes, or their ideas. Perhaps, in his alienation, fear, and epistemological and existential ignorance, man needs to find something to give him meaning and purpose in life. That which gives him such meaning, or at least that which he thinks does, even if it's only the creation itself, is what he bestows his adoration and praise upon. In short, it's what he worships. It's his god, and yet just like the wooden god that Isaiah mocks in chapter 44 this god cannot satisfy now, and in the end it cannot save because it isn't the Creator but only the creature and is therefore as fleeting and as temporal as those who worship it.

A few years ago the *Washington Post* ran an article on movie stars who had fallen into oblivion (into *hbl, ayin, efs, tohu*?). Who remembers Shelly Long, Rory Calhoun, Sally Struthers, Katherine Ross, or Mary Crosby? These were once idols—their names once burned in neon, their faces once crowded the airwaves (Mary Crosby, after all, shot J.R.!)—yet now it's all gone because in and of itself it had less endurance and meaning than the tree Isaiah's idolater worshiped. "I've long since," said Mary Crosby, "turned into a trivia question."[8]

Yet even that which endures longer than stardom doesn't satisfy either because by its nature it can't. Media mogul Ted Turner, at a speech given to the American Society of Magazine Editors, expressed the futility of being a billionaire:

> Once you make a billion dollars it's not that big of a deal. Years ago, there was a time when my stock was rising quickly. I knew how many shares of stock I had—I had only one stock, I never had time to play the market—and I figured out that if the stock hit a certain point, I was going to be a billionaire. I was still in my tiny office where I was when I was worth only a few million. I couldn't tell anyone at the office. All of my friends were working at the company—the highest paid person made about $100,000—and I was so much richer than my other friends in Atlanta that I couldn't tell them, because they'd think that I was bragging. So I went home and told my wife, and she said, "I don't care. I've got to help the kids with their homework." No one even cared. I thought bells and whistles would go off. Nothing happened at all. Having great wealth is one of the most disappointing things. It's overrated, I can tell you that. It's not as good as average sex. Average sex is better than being a billionaire.[9]

But even more importantly, these things of the world, like the tree in Isaiah 44, can't save, because they are all ultimately material, ultimately only of this world, and as the apostle John expressed so passionately, "For all that is in the world, the lust of the flesh, and the lust of the eyes, and the pride of life, is not of the Father, but is of the world. And the world passeth away, and the lust thereof: but he that doeth the will of God abideth for ever" (1 John 2:16, 17).

"Any moralist will tell you," wrote C. S. Lewis, "that the personal triumph of an athlete or of a girl at a ball is transitory: the point is to remember that an empire or a civilization is also transitory. All achievements and triumphs, in so far as they are this—worldly achievements and triumphs, will come to nothing in the end. Most scientists here join hands with theologians; the earth will not always be inhabitable. Mankind, though longer lived than men, is equally mortal. The difference is that whereas the scientists expect only a slow decay from within, we reckon with sudden interruption from without—at any moment."[10]

"But the day of the Lord will come as a thief in the night; in which the heavens shall pass away with a great noise, and the elements shall melt with fervent heat, the earth also and the works that are therein shall be burned up" (2 Peter 3:10).

The works therein—Hollywood stardom, Ted Turner's first (and last) billion, and Isaiah's idolater—will ultimately burn. All of which leads to the essential question regarding free will. No matter how many of the factors that make up our lives are beyond our control, the ultimate question is this: Do we want to go back to the oblivion out of which we came?

None of us asked to be here, so none of us have to stay, not now, not for eternity. That's the bottom line, the choice of all choices, the choice on which all other choices rest. Here's where our understanding of the final annihilation of the lost, as opposed to the demonic, nonsensical, abhorrent doctrine of eternal torment, makes such perfect sense. Only two ultimate fates await humanity: oblivion (not a tormented existence in some ever-burning hell), or eternity in bliss. Because we didn't ask to exist, God will honor our choice not to.

Yet He offers us, through Jesus Christ, not only a new and better life here but an eternal life with Him in the new heavens and the new earth that He promises through Isaiah. The choice is now, what it has always been, life or death.

"See, I have set before thee this day life and good, and death and evil" (Deuteronomy 30:15).

"I call heaven and earth to record this day against you, that I have set before you life and death, blessing and cursing: therefore choose life, that both thou and thy seed may live" (Deuteronomy 30:19).

You might not have been able to choose many of the factors of your existence now, but what Isaiah says, and teaches so poignantly, is that through the atonement wrought by the Suffering Servant, you can choose a new life, now and forever.

"Listen, listen to me, and eat well and pamper yourself in fatness. Incline your ear and come to me, and your soul will live and I will cut with you an everlasting covenant, the faithful loving kindness of David" (Isaiah 55:2, 3).

---

[1]Reinhold Niebuhr, *The Nature and Destiny of Man, Human Nature* (New York: Charles Scribner's Sons, 1964), 1:17.

[2]Gilbert Ryle, "It Was to Be," *Dilemmas* (Cambridge: Cambridge University Press, 1964).

[3]Sir James Jean, "Some Problems of Philosophy," excerpted in *Man and the Universe: The Philosopher of Science*, Saxe Commins and Robert N. Linsott, eds. (New York: Random House, 1947), 403.

[4]Bertrand Russell, *Human Society in Ethics and Politics* (New York: Mentor Books, 1955), 79.

[5]Albert Einstein, *Out of My Later Years* (London: Thames and Hudson, 1950), 27.

[6]Quoted in "The Electronic Hive: Two Views," *Harper's Magazine*, May 1994, 18, 19.

[7]The Masoretic text has the letters *ayin, vav, nun*, usually translated "iniquity." The BHS critical apparatus, citing the LXX and the Syriac, has it as *ayin, yod, nun*, transliterated here as *ayin*, the negative particle. It appears to be a scribal error, in which the *yod* was mistaken for an *ayin*, two letters that are somewhat similar looking. This probably accounts for the minor textual discrepancy.

[8]Henry Allen, "The Slippery Slope of Stardom," *Washington Post*, August 24, 1997, G8.

[9]Ted Turner, quoted in "Ted Turner's Big Letdown," *Harper's Magazine*, June 1997, 33.

[10]C. S. Lewis, *Earth's Last Night and Other Essays* (New York: Harcourt and Brace, 1987), 110.

# SIX

# The City
# of Man

*"Things fall apart; the centre cannot hold;*
*Mere anarchy is loosed upon the world,*
*The blood-dimmed tide is loosed, and everywhere*
*The ceremony of innocence is drowned;*
*The best lack all conviction, while the worst*
*Are full of passionate intensity."*
*—William Butler Yeats[1]*

The name *Isaiah* means "Salvation is of the Lord." Appropriate, considering that the book of Isaiah is about almost nothing but salvation, the salvation that comes from the Lord.

That's an important point, because at different times in history men have thought that salvation, whatever it was, whatever it meant, would have to be a man-made accomplishment if it were ever to be attained. If men were to get themselves out of the mess they had made of their existence, they'd have to roll up their sleeves, use their rational thought processes—and save themselves. And there were moments, however fleeting, ephemeral, and pathetically naive when it was believed that salvation could, indeed, be attained by works—man's works against disease, superstition, racism, poverty, immorality, and war.

One such time was the beginning years of the twentieth century, 1901, 1902, 1903. After all, decades had passed since Darwin had explained that we were progressing as a species and that if time could turn grunting Neanderthals with spears into *homo sapiens* writing Goethe's *Faustus* and Dvorak's Symphony No. 9 in E Minor, then who knew what next great step mankind would take? The major powers were at peace (Winston Churchill, in 1895, after witnessing the Spanish fighting the Cubans, said that this would be the last war in which whites would fight whites), the economy was booming, knowledge was increasing, eugenics was showing great promise (it worked fine with dogs and horses), China was still open for the gospel, and the trains were running on time.[2]

If ever mankind should have been optimistic, it was then.

"Neither the earth nor even the sun," wrote Hans Konig about those opening moments of the century, "was in the center of the universe anymore, but as Queen Victoria's chaplain, Charles Kingsley, had earlier written, 'The railroad, Cunard's liners, and the electric telegraph are . . . signs that we are, on some points at least, in harmony with the universe; that there is a mighty spirit working among us . . . the ordering and creating God.' Men and women, more than ever before or since, felt at home on earth and in control of their destiny. That natural demons of the past had been banished by reason and electricity, and the human demons of the new century were still hidden."[3]

But not for long. A week after a Bosnian terrorist named Gavrilo Princip shot an Austrian archduke in the streets of Sarajevo, the great European powers were in a war in which, within a few years, 20,000 British and Canadian soldiers would be routinely killed on a single morning in the trenches along the Somme. If mankind didn't get the message then, perhaps people got it after the Germans made lampshades and soap from Jews they stuffed in sealed rooms and gassed or after Pol Pot's killing fields in Cambodia or after an estimated 3,600,000 people in the Balkans were ethnically cleansed while

200,000 more died in the inaugural battles of what's been called "the great post-Cold War era."[4]

Obviously, there's something self-destructive about humanity, something so inherently evil that even good works often turn out bad. In *Einstein: The Life and Times,* Ronald W. Clark illustrated how even the most innocent of events can be twisted in ways never imagined by those who produced them. "When a young man approached Einstein in Prague in 1921," wrote Clark, "wanting to produce a weapon from nuclear energy based on $E=mc^2$, he was told to calm himself. 'You haven't lost anything if I don't discuss your work in detail,' Einstein said. 'Its foolishness is evident at first glance.' "[5]

Yet today man has made enough weapons from "nuclear energy based on $E=mc^2$" to leave the planet looking like a smoldering little dwarf. And human nature being what it is, it doesn't take much to imagine a Russian army security officer, tired of getting paid in stale cabbages, being lured by a desert oil colonel's petrol dollars into stealing one or two of these aging bombs either.

But even if the Russian officer can't get his hands on a few bombs, man has devised chemical and biological weapons in order to kill each other—sarin (used by the Aum Shinrikyo cult in their subway attack) which paralyzes chest muscles, causing suffocation in about fifteen minutes; VX, which in tiny doses attacks the nervous system, causing nausea, convulsions, and seizures before killing victims; Ricin (made from the castor bean), which causes blood poisoning that leads to the collapse of the circulatory system in a slow, painful death; or Anthrax spores, which spread through the air and cause death within five to seven days. Men have used some of these before and no doubt will again.

"Officials in Washington," said *Time,* "are deeply worried about what some of them call a 'strategic crime.' By that they mean the merging of the output from a government's arsenals, like Saddam's biological weapons, with a group of semi-independent terrorists, like radical Islamist groups, who might slip such bio-weapons into the

U.S. and use them. It wouldn't take much. This is the poor man's atomic bomb. A gram of anthrax culture contains a trillion spores, theoretically enough for 100 million fatal doses. . . . And Saddam has produced anthrax in large amounts."[6]

Thus, whatever optimism pervaded the opening of the twentieth century, the obvious question at its close shouldn't be, Can mankind save himself? but Who will save mankind *from himself?*

The answer is found, again and again, in Isaiah:

> Behold, *God is my salvation.* I will trust and I will not be afraid, for the Lord is my strength and song, and he has become my salvation (Isaiah 12:2, italics supplied).

> The Lord has laid bare His holy arm before the eyes of all the nations and all the ends of the earth shall see *the salvation of our God* (Isaiah 52:10, italics supplied).

> And one will say on that day, "Behold, this is our God; we have waited for Him, and He has saved us. This is the Lord; we have waited for Him. We will be glad and rejoice in *His salvation*" (Isaiah 25:9, italics supplied).

> My righteousness is near; *my salvation* has gone forth (Isaiah 51:5, italics supplied).

> Lift up your eyes toward heaven and look to the earth beneath, for heaven as smoke will vanish and the earth as a garment will wear out, and its inhabitants in a like manner will die. But *my salvation* will be forever and my righteousness will not be abolished. For the moth will eat them like a garment, and the worm will eat them like wool, but righteousness will be forever and my salvation from generation to generation (Isaiah 51:6-8, italics supplied).

Thus says the Lord, Keep justice and do judgment, because *my salvation* is near to come and my righteousness to be revealed (Isaiah 56:1, italics supplied).

I will greatly rejoice in the Lord; my soul will be joyful in the Lord, because *He has dressed me in garments of salvation* and covered me in robes of righteousness (Isaiah 61:10, italics supplied).

Though the word *salvation* appears about 158 times in all sixty-six books of the KJV Bible (an average of less than three times per book), twenty-six are in Isaiah alone (which is even more remarkable considering that the word is used only forty-six times in the entire New Testament). Salvation, obviously, is a major theme in Isaiah, and as the preceding verses show (and even as Isaiah's name proclaims)—"Salvation is of the Lord."

The word usually translated "salvation" comes from a root of three letters, *yod, shin, ayin, (yahshah)* from which the name *Jesus* (*Yeshuah* in Hebrew) is derived. The root means to "deliver" or "save," and it occurs fifty-six times in Isaiah, a much higher percentage than in any other biblical book except Psalms (136 times). In a majority of cases, the verb appears in the hiphil (*hosia*), or causative form, which usually implies that something *causes* deliverance or salvation to something else. The emphasis is on the subject that does the act of saving. And in Isaiah, that subject, that causative agent of salvation or deliverance, in every instance, is the Lord. (Even the word *Savior* is often derived from the hiphil of *yahshah*).

For the Lord is our judge, the Lord is our lawgiver, the Lord is our king. *He will save us* (Isaiah 33:22, italics supplied).

*Israel shall be saved in the Lord* with an everlasting salvation (Isaiah 45:17, italics supplied).

And one will say on that day, "Behold, this is our God; we have waited for Him, *and He has saved us"* (Isaiah 25:9, italics supplied).

I, even I, am the Lord, and there is no Saviour besides me (Isaiah 43:11).

"Behold, *the hand of the Lord is not too short to save,* nor is his ear too heavy to hear" (Isaiah 59:1, italics supplied).

Say to the fearful, "Be strong, don't be afraid; behold, your God comes with vengeance, God with recompense; *He will come and save you"* (Isaiah 35:4, italics supplied).

For I am the Lord thy God, the holy One of Israel, *your Saviour* (Isaiah 43:3, italics supplied).

"In prophetic literature," says the *Theological Dictionary of the Old Testament,* "the proper subject of *hosia* is always God. . . . There are no exceptions."[7]

All over Isaiah, the theme is the same: God alone can save us; we can't do it ourselves, nor can we count on others to do it for us—and only disappointment and disaster await those who try. In fact, Isaiah is so heavy-laden with the promise and hope of God's salvation for us that the root word for "redeem" (from which "Redeemer" comes) appears about twenty times in Isaiah, a disproportionately high number considering that in the remaining thirty-eight books of the Hebrew Bible it occurs only sixty times.

Fear not, worm of Jacob, and men of Israel. I, I will help you, says the Lord, and thy *Redeemer,* the Holy one of Israel (Isaiah 41:14, italics supplied).

But now, thus says the Lord, the one who created you, Jacob, and who formed you Israel. Do not fear, because I have *redeemed* you; I have called you by name; you are mine (Isaiah 43:1, italics supplied).

I have blotted out as a thick cloud your transgressions, and like a cloud your sins. Return to me, because I have *redeemed* you (Isaiah 44:22, italics supplied).

Thus says the Lord, the king of Israel and His *Redeemer*, the Lord of Hosts: I am the first, I am the last and besides me there is no other God (Isaiah 44:6, italics supplied).

Thus says the Lord, your *Redeemer*, the one who formed you from the womb (Isaiah 44:24, italics supplied).

Our *Redeemer*, the Lord of hosts is His name, the Holy one of Israel (Isaiah 47:4, italics supplied).

Thus says the Lord, your *Redeemer,* the Holy One of Israel (Isaiah 48:17, italics supplied).

I the Lord am your Saviour and your *Redeemer,* the Mighty One of Jacob (Isaiah 49:26, italics supplied).

For your Creator is your husband, the Lord of Hosts is His name; and your *Redeemer,* the Holy One of Israel shall be called the God of all the earth (Isaiah 54:5, italics supplied).

For you are our Father, for even if Abraham didn't know us and Israel did not acknowledge us, you, Lord, are our Father, our *Redeemer*; your name is from everlasting (Isaiah 63:16, italics supplied).

And if ever a people needed redemption or salvation, it was God's church during Isaiah's ministry, a time of great social, moral, and political upheaval for those who professed to worship "the Holy One of Israel." From without and within, God's people were being ravaged, and, and, as always, their worst enemies were themselves. At any moment they could be destroyed by the mighty Assyrian nation, which was at its apogee. Samaria, to the north, had already fallen to the Assyrians in 722 B.C. Fears became real when Sennacherib invaded Judah in 701 B.C. and destroyed most of the major cities all the way down to Egypt.

Meanwhile, the kings who ruled during Isaiah's watch were some of the worst compromisers, including Ahaz, who introduced pagan practices into the temple grounds itself, and his grandson Mannasah, who burned children as sacrifices to pagan gods and (according to tradition) sawed Isaiah in half.

Isaiah spent his life preaching to a people who closed their ears to his pleading, and as a result disaster after disaster struck. Whatever their profession, the professed followers of the Lord were immersed in idolatry, false worship, and injustice. "The people forsook God and His ways of righteousness. . . . Everywhere there was a miscarriage of justice, for magistrates judged for reward and rulers were primarily interested in personal gain. Greed, avarice, and vice were the order of the day. As the rich became richer the poor became poorer, and many sank into the depths of poverty and were reduced to the status of slaves."[8]

And yet amid all this Isaiah repeatedly gives promises of hope, of deliverance, of salvation—not just in a temporal sense but in an eternal one. While the people were in apostasy, while the rulers were corrupt, while justice was forsaken, while military foes were raping their daughters and dragging off their sons to captivity—the Lord through Isaiah gave some of the most poignant, beautiful, and powerful truths regarding the salvation and redemption to be wrought out by the Savior and Redeemer both at His first and second comings, even though these promises were often immersed in, and at times almost indistinguishable from, the local historical events.

For example, one moment Isaiah could be talking about a confederacy between Rezin, king of Syria, and Pekah, king of Israel, against Judah (Isaiah 7:1-9), and the next moment he gives a Messianic prophecy about Jesus: "Therefore the Lord Himself will give to you a sign. Behold, a virgin will conceive and bear a son, and you will call his name Immanuel" (verse 14). In chapter 9, Isaiah presents this beautiful prophecy regarding Christ: "For a son is born to us; a child is given to us, and the government will be upon His shoulder, and His name shall be called Wonderful, Counselor, God Almighty, Everlasting Father, the Prince of Peace" (Isaiah 9:6). And then he immediately talks about such local issues as Ephraim (verse 9) and Rezin of Samaria (verse 11). Chapter 10 continues for thirty-four verses about the Assyrian invasions (verse 5), about Samaria (verse 11), about Migron and Michmash (verse 28), about the "inhabitants of Gebim" (verse 31), and about Lebanon (verse 34), when verse 1 of the next chapter immediately bursts into a prophecy about Christ: "And there shall come forth a rod from the stem of Jesse, and a branch from its roots will grow. And the Spirit of the Lord will rest upon Him, a spirit of wisdom and understanding, a spirit of counsel and might, and a spirit of the knowledge and the fear of God" (Isaiah 11:1, 2). Almost the whole of chapter 63 is Isaiah writing about the sins of the Hebrew nation—the rebellion (verse 2), the false worship (verse 3), the eating of pig meat (verse 4), blasphemy (verse 7), and the punishment that will come (verses 11-13)—when he then explodes into this wonderful promise of a whole new existence: "For, behold, I will create a new heavens and a new earth, and the former things will not be remembered or come into mind" (verse 17).

What Isaiah shows is that local events can often be understood as "types" or examples of what God wants to do on a grand scale. The judgments on Israel are prophetic types of a time when God will judge the whole world; the promise to the Hebrew nation of salvation and redemption from local enemies can be prophetic types of the time when God will ultimately save His people through the ministry of Jesus at both His comings. Understanding this principle can help make great sense of classical prophecies that can seem incredibly confusing.[9]

In Matthew 24, Jesus illustrated this principle when He wove together a description of the destruction of Jerusalem, which would come before the end of the century, with details of the Second Coming, which occurs at the end of the world. In His discourse, Jesus drew no sharp line of demarcation between both events; instead He ties them into one:

When ye therefore shall see the abomination of desolation, spoken of by Daniel the prophet, stand in the holy place, (whoso readeth, let him understand:) Then let them which be in Judaea flee into the mountains: Let him which is on the housetop not come down to take any thing out of his house: Neither let him which is in the field return back to take his clothes. And woe unto them that are with child, and to them that give suck in those days! But pray ye that your flight be not in the winter, neither on the sabbath day: For then shall be great tribulation, such as was not since the beginning of the world to this time, no, nor ever shall be (Matthew 24:15-21).

Wrote Ellen White:

Christ's words had been spoken in the hearing of a large number of people; but when He was alone, Peter, John, James, and Andrew came to Him as He sat upon the Mount of Olives. "Tell us," they said, "when shall these things be? and what shall be the sign of Thy coming, and of the end of the world?" Jesus did not answer His disciples by taking up separately the destruction of Jerusalem and the great day of His coming. He mingled the description of these two events. Had He opened to His disciples future events as He beheld them, they would have been unable to endure the sight. In mercy to them He blended the description of the two great crises, leaving the disciples to study out the meaning for themselves. When He referred to the destruction of Jerusalem, His prophetic words reached beyond that event to the final conflagration in that day when the Lord shall rise out of His place to punish the world for their iniquity, when the earth shall disclose her blood, and shall no more cover her slain. This entire discourse was given, not for the disciples only, but for those who should live in the last scenes of this earth's history.[10]

Thus, with reference after reference to salvation from the pen of Isaiah the prophet, even amid the turmoil in which he lived, the thing that should reach out of the pages, grab our heads, and shake us out of our stupor, fears, and doubts is that no matter whether we live in eighth-century Palestine, with all its corruption, suffering, and insecurity, or in twentieth-century America, with all its corruption, suffering, and insecurity as well—God can save and deliver all who are willing to be saved and delivered either in this life, in the next, or both.

We might not live under the threat of an Assyrian or later Babylonian invasion, but what we do live under can ruin our lives, homes, and families just as efficiently and thoroughly as the swords of Sennacherib's troops. Each of us is just one twisted, corrupt, selfish sinner crammed with 5.8 billion other twisted, corrupt, and selfish sinners on a polluted planet whose surface is mostly uninhabitable saltwater. No matter who we are, no matter how wealthy, happy, and contented, nature still aims to kill us and everyone whom we love, either quickly or slowly, tortuously, and without remorse—and

it always succeeds, one way or another. No matter how well we orga-
nize and plan our lives, careers, finances, and families, so much lurks
out there that can snatch it all away or damage, twist, and even turn it
against us and ruin us both inside and out until, as Nietzsche wrote,
"Your soul will be dead even before your body."[11] If, as Mark Twain
said, only death and taxes are sure in this life, then that leaves a lot of
other things—things we love, cherish, and need—no more certain
than a winning lottery ticket.

"Modern attitudes were expressed with great succinctness by
Sartre," wrote Dr. Glenn Tinder, "when he said, through a character
in his novel *Nausea*, that '*anything* can happen, *anything*.' The modern mood is one of radical insecurity; nothing is so senseless or cata-
strophic that we can assume it will not befall us."[12]

Anything can happen because, indeed, anything and everything
has happened—if not to us personally (at least not yet), then to someone we know and, of course, all the time to millions we don't know.
Thus, with so much pain, suffering, fear, dread, and angst all around
us, what gives us the right to be at peace, or to even think we should
be? How can we be anything other than full of dread and pain when
11 million children under the age of five die every year (that's more
than 30,000 a day!)? How can we smile when a thousand people will
kill themselves today? How can we be content when 100 million
children live on the streets of the world's cities or when in Bangladesh
a flood killed 138,000 people in one day?

"What were you doing," asked writer Anne Dillard, "on April 30,
1991, when a series of waves drowned 138,000 people? Where were
you when you first heard the astounding, heartbreaking news? Who
told you? What, seriatim, were your sensations? Who did you tell?
Did you weep? Did your anguish last days or weeks?"[13]

The point is simple: We're in a world that in and of itself leads to
tragedy for everyone; a world where all the great political causes, all
the great "isms" (that once held out so much promise) have failed;
a world where, according to the second law of thermodynamics,

everything is moving toward collapse, entropy, heat, death; a world that by its very nature needs to be saved and yet a world in which man—with all his technology and science—can only prolong the agony but never end it.

That's why the message of Isaiah is as pertinent now, in the twentieth century A.D., as it was in the eighth century B.C.—and that message is that all attempts to save ourselves will crash and burn. Though writing in the context of the French revolution, Page Smith captures the essence of the dilemma that occurs when man seeks answers only in himself or in his own materialistic devising: "For the Garden of Eden, the philosophers of the French Revolution offered the relatively brief days of high Greek and Athenian culture; for bliss in heaven, they offered bliss on earth; for original sin, they proposed the natural goodness of men and women; for faith, they substituted reason; for Christian teaching, science; for the triune God, nature. Such was the religion of the city of man."[14]

And that's the city so many of us live in today, the city of man, a city that doesn't extend beyond itself, where life remains a brutal, fruitless endeavor, no matter how man—with his "high Greek and Athenian culture," reason, and natural goodness—tries to make it otherwise. In fact, so often the attempt to make it otherwise is exactly what makes it so brutal and fruitless. The situation is one of utter and sheer helplessness and absurdity—and the sooner that cold realization creeps through our bodies in a wave of fear, even panic, the better off we are, because only then can we know that if we're ever to be saved, it must be from God alone, who time and again through His servant Isaiah makes that plea to look beyond this life, to look beyond what we have here alone, to something better, to something eternal, to something holy and righteous, to something beyond what man can do because man cannot do it.

There's something in us that cries out for permanence, for meaning, for stability, and yet all around, everything in nature, in science, in common sense and reason alone tells us that we can't have stability or permanence. That is one reason why the world is filled with despair, lunacy, mental illness, drug addiction, and alcoholism (if you can't solve the problem, then at least numb the pain). "Either there is some support for our being," wrote Richard Bernstein, "a fixed foundation for our knowledge, or we cannot escape the forces of darkness that envelop us with madness, with intellectual and moral chaos."[15] And what Isaiah is saying is that without the supernatural intervention of God, this dismal, hopeless message of nature, science, common sense, and reason has got it right, and all there is are the forces of darkness, madness, and chaos.

Yet how fortunate that as Christians we know that science, nature, common sense, and reason don't have the last word. God's Word is the last word. Perhaps the greatest message of salvation and hope in Isaiah is in chapter 59, where verse after verse depicts the sins of God's people—hands defiled with blood (verse 3), lying (verse 4), violence (verse 6), thoughts of iniquity (verse 7), injustice (verse 9), transgression against God (verse 13), and so forth. Yet, despite this, the Lord is still willing to save them, still willing to cover them, still willing to give them the promises of eternity but only if they will accept Him and turn from their ways. "Behold, the hand of the Lord isn't too short that it cannot save, nor His ear too heavy that it cannot hear" (verse 1). "And the Redeemer will come to Zion, and unto them that turn from transgression in Jacob, says the Lord" (verse 20).

The message to us is that no matter how bad we are, no matter how much we have transgressed, no matter how many times we or our loved ones have scorned His mercy, His grace, His law—the Lord is still willing to save us, still willing to redeem us, still willing to give us all those things that He has time and again promised even though Isaiah's depictions of the sins of the people show that they— like us—are unworthy. But that's what Isaiah, the Bible, indeed, the whole human condition is about—it's about us spitting in the face of the One who is constantly pleading with us to turn away from the things that cannot save, that cannot satisfy, and that cannot redeem. The Romans alone didn't spit in the face of Christ; Adam did, and we've been doing it, too, ever since. And yet He still turns that face to us in love and beckons us to look to Him and be saved.

But how can we be saved? How can Isaiah—amid all this corruption, sin, and evil—constantly hold out the promise of eternal salvation, of redemption, of deliverance? The answer is found within many of the texts themselves:

My *righteousness* is near; my *salvation* has gone forth (Isaiah 51:5, italics supplied).

Lift up your eyes toward heaven and look to the earth beneath, for heaven as smoke will vanish and the earth as a garment will wear out, and its inhabitants in a like manner will die. But my *salvation* will be forever and my *righteousness* will not be abolished. For the moth will eat them like a garment, and the worm will eat them like wool, but *righteousness* will be forever and my *salvation* from generation to generation (Isaiah 51:6-8, italics supplied).

Thus says the Lord, "Keep justice and do judgment, because my *salvation* is near to come and my *righteousness* to be revealed" (Isaiah 56:1, italics supplied).

I will greatly rejoice in the Lord; my soul will be joyful in the Lord, because He has dressed me in garments of *salvation* and covered me in robes of *righteousness* (Isaiah 61:10, italics supplied).

I bring near my *righteousness*; it will not be far off; my *salvation* will not tarry. I will put *salvation* in Israel for my glory (Isaiah 46:13, italics supplied).

In each verse, "salvation" parallels "righteousness," and in each one, it is *God's* salvation (the salvation He bestows upon us) that is linked to *His* righteousness. In other words, the salvation that the Lord constantly offers to His people, this evil, backslidden people, is tied to His righteousness, which is the only reason they can be saved.

"Salvation" and "righteousness" appear almost synonymously in these verses. This parallel between "righteousness" and "salvation" appears less than twenty times in the whole Bible, with ten of them in Isaiah alone (all the other OT appearances being in Psalms). Once the parallel appears in the New Testament: "For with the heart man believeth unto *righteousness;* and with the mouth confession is made unto *salvation"* (Romans 10:10, italics supplied).

This parallel between "salvation" and "righteousness" in Isaiah helps answer the question of how God can redeem His people. It is God's righteousness that provides the means of salvation—the reason why even amid all the apostasy, evil, sin, and unrighteousness, God can still save souls. No wonder salvation comes only from Him and why all man's attempts to save himself are doomed to degenerate into the same hopelessness and futility that has marked each effort from the first time man tried to save himself and will continue to do so up until the very end, when all of man's efforts, achievements, and exploits will be swept away into the infinite nothingness from which they sprang, and the only thing remaining are those saved in the righteousness of God.

[1]William Butler Yeats, "The Second Coming," *The Ways of the Poem,* Josephine Miles, ed. (Old Tappan, N. J.: Prentice Hall, 1961), 415, 416.
[2]Said Reverend Newell Hillis to his Brooklyn congregation in 1900: "Laws are becoming more just, rulers humane; music is becoming sweeter and books wiser."
A major American newspaper, on December 31, 1899, had this to say about the pervading optimism: "Tomorrow we enter upon the last year of a century that is marked by a greater progress in all that pertains to the material well-being and enlightenment of mankind than in all the previous history of the race," *New York Times.*
[3]Hans Konig, "Notes on the Twentieth Century," *Atlantic Monthly,* September 1997, 90.

[4]Mark Danner, "Still Living in a Cold-War World," *Harper's Magazine,* December 1997, 19.
[5]Ronald W. Clark, *Einstein: His Life and Times* (New York: Avon Books, 1984), 135.
[6]"America the Vulnerable," *Time,* November 24, 1997, 50, 51.
[7]*Theological Dictionary of the Old Testament* (Grand Rapids: Wm. B. Eerdmans, 1990), 6:455.
[8]*SDA Bible Commentary* (Hagerstown, Md.: Review and Herald, 1955), 4:89.
[9]"Thus, we find," wrote Hans LaRondelle, "the characteristic feature of classical prophecy is its *dual focus* on the near and on the far, without any differentiation in time. It teaches us that the God of Israel is the God of history. He is the King who comes both in history and at the end of human history. His coming brings the end of this evil age, in order to restore the kingdom of God on our planet through Jesus Christ. (From an unpublished manuscript titled *How to Understand the End-Time Prophecies of the Bible,* Hans LaRondelle, Part 1, p. 9.
[10]*The Desire of Ages,* 628.
[11]Friedrich Nietzsche, *Thus Spake Zarathustra* (New York: Penguin Classics, 1969), 48.
[12]Glenn Tinder, "Augustine's World and Ours," *First Things,* December 1997, 38.
[13]Anne Dillard, "The Wreck of Times," *Harper's Magazine,* January 1998, 53.
[14]Page Smith, *Rediscovering Christianity* (New York: St. Martin's Press, 1994), 104.
[15]Richard J. Bernstein, *Beyond Objectivism and Relativism: Science, Hermeneutics, and Praxis* (Philadelphia: University of Pennsylvania Press, 1983), 18.

# SEVEN

# What God Cannot Do

*"We do not put the life of God and the foreknowledge of God under any necessity when we say that God must live and must know all things. Neither do we lessen His power when we say that He cannot die or be deceived. . . . It is precisely because He is omnipotent that for Him some things are impossible."*
—*St. Augustine*[1]

"All men by nature desire to know," wrote Aristotle at the beginning of his *Metaphysics*."[2]

"Our urge to know is so great," wrote paleontologist Stephen Jay Gould, "but our common errors cut so deep"[3] (Gould, whose life is based on error, should know).

This human desire for knowledge can be good or bad. In Eden, of course, it was bad, leading to a disaster that has affected every moment of human existence, from then to now, thousands of years after Adam first desired to know "good and evil."

But men still desire knowledge, especially about themselves and the world around them. From the beginning of recorded history, people have been asking, "What's it all about? What is the basic structure of the world? What makes it tick? Why does nature do this as opposed to that?"

From the ancient Greek Thales (who said that everything was water) through modern physics (which says that everything is quarks) humans have been trying to understand the prime nature of the universe. And yet, as far as science has come, it still hasn't discovered that basic principle, that Theory of Everything (TOE), a complete mathematical description of the world in one simple, neat formula. And that's because, though a TOE exists, it's not written in numbers; it's written in blood, the blood of Christ—and its basic message is "God is love" (1 John 4:16).

But what does that mean—"God is love"? Love, after all, is an emotion, a neuro-hormonal response of the limbic system, or even a principle, and God is certainly more than any of these. If the Bible said, "God loves" or that "Love is a manifestation of the character of God," it would be easier to understand. But Scripture says "God *is* love"—a statement that is, at best, problematic.

Whatever the statement "God is love" may mean, some conclusions can be drawn from it. One is that if God is love, then there are some things that God cannot do. After all, Paul wrote, "[I]n hope of eternal life, which God, *that cannot lie,* promised before the world began" (Titus 1:2, italics supplied). According to Paul, God cannot lie. There are some things, then, that God cannot do, and this is especially true if He is love.

A man who loves his neighbor, yet lusts after that neighbor's wife, will be less likely to steal that wife than he would be if he didn't love that neighbor. In other words, love limits his options.

It's the same with God. Because He is love, there are some things He cannot do—such as force His creatures to love Him in return, because love that is forced is not, and cannot be, love. Love by its very definition cannot be coerced, because if it is, it's no longer love. Even God cannot create a love that is forced, any more than He can create a circle whose border isn't everywhere equidistant to its center. Love, to be love, must be free, just as a circle, to be a circle, must have a border everywhere equidistant to its center. The moment love is not free, it's not love. Just as the moment the border of a circle isn't equidistant to its center, it's no longer a circle.

To love God, then, we must have the option not to love Him. The negative possibility must exist in order for the positive one to exist as well. It's as if the very definition of love must include the option not to love. Love can't exist without the possibility of not loving, which explains why Lucifer, as well as Adam and Eve, though created perfect, could fall. Love demanded that they be given the option of not loving, a choice they opted for.

In *Early Writings*, Ellen White wrote about inhabitants on another planet who were "noble, majestic, and lovely" and who "bore the express image of Jesus." She also said that in their midst grew two trees, and that though these inhabitants "had power to eat of both,"[4] they were forbidden to eat from one. Here, as in Eden, as in heaven with the angels, the option to disobey must exist, otherwise love couldn't exist either.

There is, however, a flip side: Whatever limits love has placed on God, in the sense that love by its nature is a restricting element, love has also opened up fascinating prospects that could not otherwise exist.

How?

From a human perspective, however much love might stop us from some actions, it compels us to do things that wouldn't be done were it not for love. How many wonderful, gallant, self-denying actions have been done by those motivated by nothing but love? All through history, both sacred and profane, numerous examples exist of people sacrificing themselves solely out of love for others. In short, love drives people to do things, often good things, that they would not do were it not for love. Therefore, if love can compel weak, sinful, selfish, fallen human beings to do wonderful acts, what could it motivate God to do?

"For God so loved the world, that he gave his only begotten Son, that whosoever believeth in him should not perish, but have everlasting life" (John 3:16).

"But God commendeth his love toward us, in that, while we were yet sinners, Christ died for us" (Romans 5:8).

"Hereby perceive we the love of God, because he laid down his life for us: and we ought to lay down our lives for the brethren" (1 John 3:16).

"Now our Lord Jesus Christ himself, and God, even our Father, which hath loved us, and hath given us everlasting consolation and good hope through grace" (2 Thessalonians 2:16).

The point is amazingly simple yet profound beyond human reasoning—the same love that forced God to create us free is the same love that motivated Him to die on the cross. Maybe love, by its nature as love, required that God create us free, but it didn't require Him to die on the cross. Love can't exist without freedom; the very definition of love demands it. But there's nothing inherent in love that *demands* what happened at the cross. Christ had to freely choose to go, or it wouldn't be love that motivated Him. Christ went to the cross not because He had to, but because He loved us.

Love is the heart of the gospel, and it's the heart of the message of Isaiah, the gospel prophet, which is why one of the clearest, most explicit and concentrated expositions of the gospel, of what Christ's love motivated Him to do—occurs in Isaiah chapter 53. Though the gospel appears all through Isaiah's book (as does Creation, which makes sense since creation and redemption are so linked), chapter 53 gives the most vivid explanation of Christ's substitutionary atonement to appear anywhere in the Bible, Paul's writing included. In Isaiah 53, the Bible presents one of its greatest revelations of what true love is all about: the total self-sacrifice of one for another.

Though Isaiah 53 is rich in numerous themes, the following verses, culled from the chapter, concentrate on one specific aspect: what Isaiah says Christ did for us at the cross:

"Surely He has carried our infirmities and borne our suffer-ings. . . . And he was profaned from our transgressions and He was crushed from our iniquities, and the punishment of our peace was upon Him . . . and the Lord has put on him the iniquity of all of us . . . because of the transgression of my people He was smitten. . . . You shall make His life an offering for sin . . . with His knowledge will My Righteous Servant justify many; and their iniquities He will bear . . . He carried the sins of many and made intercession for the transgressors."

Each of these phrases, sequenced in verses 4-12 of chapter 53, depict one aspect or another of Christ's death in our stead, the ultimate expression of God's love and a theme that will never be exhausted throughout all eternity, much less fully grasped by sinful finite minds in the spasm of time in which they cogitate upon the earth. Nowhere, even in Paul's writings, is there such a single-minded concentration dealing with Christ's work of vicarious atonement—a truth that all human science, reason, philosophy, logic, and study can never re-veal—a truth so important that it had to be spoon-fed to us through written revelation. Here, hundreds of pages and thousands of verses before the Christian era began, Isaiah lays the foundation of why those who follow Christ should exude a hope for a future that far transcends anything that anyone could ever derive from this world alone, no matter all the carnal resources at his disposal.

To begin, Isaiah, with two broad, wide sweeps, presents in verse 6 the universal problem of mankind (sin) and the universal solution (the cross): "All of us like sheep have gone astray; we have turned, each man, to his own way; and the Lord has put on him the iniquity of all of us." How fascinating that both the problem and the solution can be traced back to one of the most universal statements in Scrip-ture: "God is love." Love demanded that we be free, even at the risk of sin; and love motivated Christ to take on Himself the penalty of that sin so that we can remain free.

The Hebrew word for "all of us" (*culanu*) who went astray, is the exact word used when Isaiah wrote that on Him was put the iniquity of "all of us" (*culanu*). In other words, no matter how bad and wide-spread the problem (sin), the solution (the Cross) dealt with it completely. Paul, centuries after Isaiah, explained the same theme: "If, because of one man's [Adam's] trespass, death reigned through that one man, much more will those who receive the abundance of grace and the free gift of righteousness reign in life through the one man Jesus Christ" (Romans 5:17, RSV). All of us, no matter our sins, are offered that "free gift of righteousness."

Verse 6 presents the great dichotomy of Christianity: the innocent suffering for the guilty, the greatest expression of God's love. Though Isaiah 53 only hints at the sinlessness of the Savior ("because he had done no violence, nor was deceit in his mouth" [verse 9]), the *substitutionary* aspect of what happened to Him consumes the chapter. The word in verse 6 for "put on" Him comes from a Hebrew root meaning "to meet," "to encounter," "to reach." In this specific text, the word appears in the *hiphil*, or causative, form, which means the verse says that though all of us have sinned, the Lord *caused* that sin (that is, the sin of "all of us") "to meet," "to encounter," "to reach" Jesus. In short, God caused our sin to be "put on" Him.

Isaiah repeats that crucial theme from another perspective, this time in verse 12: "And He [Christ] *carried* the sins of many" (italics supplied). The verb translated "carried" (from the Hebrew root *nasa*) appears more than six hundred times in Scripture, usually meaning "to lift," "to bear," "to carry."

Interestingly enough, after the sin of the golden calf, Moses—interceding for Israel before the Lord—exclaimed, "But now, if you will forgive their sins, but if not, blot me out from your book, which you have written" (Exodus 32:32). The word *forgive* also comes from *nasa*, "to bear" or "to carry," so the verse could have been translated "But now, if you will *carry* [or *bear*] their sins, but if not, blot me out from your book, which you have written" (Exodus 32:32).

Was Moses asking God Himself to bear the sins of his people?

Exactly! And the Lord, centuries later, answered that request: Jesus—the Lord Himself—bore those sins on the cross, just as Isaiah depicted. In fact, when Peter wrote, "Who [Christ] his own self bare our sins in his own body on the tree, that we, being dead to sins, should live unto righteousness: by whose stripes ye were healed" (1 Peter 2:24), he used concepts and imagery directly from Isaiah 53.

Other verses teach this same idea of God Himself bearing sin as the means of forgiving sinners. "And the Lord passed by before him [Moses] and the Lord proclaimed, 'The Lord God, merciful and gracious, patient and abundant in mercy and truth, keeping mercy for thousands, forgiving iniquity, transgression, and sin" (Exodus 34:6, 7). "Forgiving iniquity" could just as easily have been translated "bearing iniquity" (from *nasa*). Job, amid the rubble of tragedy, called out to the Lord, "Why don't you pardon [from *nasa*] my transgression, and take away mine iniquity? For now I shall sleep in the dust" (Job 7:21).

This concept of someone else bearing the sins of the guilty (known as substitutionary atonement) is taught in the earthly sanctuary service. In Leviticus 10, for instance, Moses said to the priest, "Why have you not eaten the sin offering in the holy place, seeing it is most holy, and God has given it you *to bear* [from *nasa*] the iniquity of the congregation, to *make atonement* for them before the Lord?" (italics supplied). Here, "bearing iniquity" is parallel to "making atonement."

No wonder, then, that Isaiah 53—so heavily laden with substitutionary theology—reflects the language of the earthly sanctuary service. Verse 10—"You shall make His life an offering for sin"—makes sense only in the context of the sanctuary, where innocent lives (goats, calves, bulls, etc.) were slain as the means of "atonement" for the transgressor. Here the Hebrew word for "an offering" means "a guilt offering" (see Leviticus 5:19; 7:5), and the verse could be translated, "When you make his life a guilt-offering." (Young's *Literal Translation* has it like this, "If his soul doth make an offering for guilt.") However translated, the message is clear: Christ paid with

His life for the sins of the guilty.

So fundamental is this idea of Jesus dying for our sins that it's repeated, in another fashion, in verse 8: "He was taken from prison and judgment: and who will speak of his generation? Because he was cut off out of the land of the living, and *because of the transgression of my people He was smitten*" (italics supplied). While most of chapter 53 deals with Christ's sufferings and death in the broad, universal sense of what He accomplished by His actions, verses 7-9 deal specifically with the physical events surrounding his death—He didn't open His mouth, He was brought from prison, He was with the rich in His death, etc. Yet even amid these details Isaiah stresses what it's all about: The people sinned and He, the Suffering Servant, was punished in their stead. Again, whatever limits love placed on God in one sense, it certainly motivated Him to act, and Isaiah, centuries before these events, revealed what those acts were and why He performed them.

In verse 4—"Surely he hath carried our grief [literally "sickness"] and borne our pains"—Christ's vicarious suffering is repeated with a different slant. The word for "carried" is *nasa,* while "bore" comes from a Hebrew root used in the context of heavy, burden-bearing work. In the following text, the term *forced labor* is from the same word translated "carried" in Isaiah 53:4— "The man Jeroboam was very able, and when Solomon saw that the young man was industrious he gave him charge over all the forced labor of the house of Joseph" (1 Kings 11:28, RSV).

It's fascinating, too, that in the previous verse—where Jesus was described "a man of pains and acquainted with grief [or sickness]"— the nouns for "pain" and "grief" are the same ones that the next verse uses to describe what Jesus bore and carried in our behalf. Thus, He was a man of pains and infirmities because He took our pains and infirmities on Himself. "When the even was come," wrote Matthew, "they brought unto him many that were possessed with devils: and he cast out the spirits with his word, and healed all that were sick:

That it might be fulfilled which was spoken by Esaias the prophet, saying, Himself took our infirmities, and bare our sicknesses" (Matthew 8:16, 17). By his acts of healing, Jesus in small ways already began the work that would climax at the cross, where He became so completely associated with sin and all the infirmities and guilt it brings (God "made him to be sin for us" —2 Corinthians 5:21) that He would die the second death, the ultimate and complete legal punishment for sin so we don't have to ourselves.

That's why Isaiah writes, "He was profaned for our transgression, He was crushed for our iniquities, and the punishment of our peace was upon him " (verse 5). The last phrase could be translated "upon him was the chastisement that made us whole" (RSV). Again, Jesus was the sin-bearer, suffering from our transgression and iniquities, and from that substitution we are forgiven, made right, and even justified before God.

In fact, the verse that gives the best *theological* summary of the chapter is verse 11: "With His knowledge will My Righteous Servant justify many; and their iniquities He will bear." Theology can't get much simpler. The "many" who accept Christ are justified because Jesus, the "Righteous Servant," has borne "their iniquities."

What's crucial is that this verse helps bring to light the issue touched on in the previous chapter, and that is the numerous times Isaiah linked righteousness to salvation.

My *righteousness* is near; my *salvation* has gone forth (Isaiah 51:5, italics supplied).

Lift up your eyes toward heaven and look to the earth beneath, for heaven as smoke will vanish and the earth as a garment will wear out, and its inhabitants in a like manner will die. But my *salvation* will be forever and my *righteousness* will not be abolished. For the moth will eat them like a garment, and the worm will eat them like wool, but *righteousness* will be forever and my *salvation* from generation to generation (Isaiah 51:6, 7, italics supplied).

Thus says the Lord, "Keep justice and do judgment, because my *salvation* is near to come and my *righteousness* to be revealed" (Isaiah 56:1, italics supplied).

I will greatly rejoice in the Lord; my soul will be joyful in the Lord, because He has dressed me in garments of *salvation* and covered me in robes of *righteousness* (Isaiah 61:10, italics supplied).

I bring near my *righteousness*; it will not be far off; my *salvation* will not tarry. I will put salvation in Israel for my glory (Isaiah 46:13, italics supplied).

The word translated "justify" in Isaiah 53:11 ("My Righteous Servant will *justify* many") comes from the same Hebrew root (*zdk*) that is translated "righteousness" in these other verses. Justification, the foundation of salvation, is inseparable from righteousness. Besides "to be righteous" (*zdk*) also means "to be just." The standard Brown-Driver-Briggs-Gesenius Hebrew lexicon gives the follow definitions of the verb root *zdk:* "be justified . . . justify . . . be just, righteous . . . make to appear righteous." In verse 11, the verb appears in the *hiphil* form ("to cause to be righteous"), which the same lexicon translates: "declare righteous, justify . . . vindicate the cause of, save . . . make righteous, turn to righteousness."

Isaiah 53 says that "my righteous [from *zdk*] servant will justify [from *zdk*] many." How? The rest of the verse helps answer that question when it says that "their iniquities he will bear."

Here's the gospel: Jesus took our iniquities upon Himself. He Himself bore the legal punishment that sin brings. Because God is a God of justice, He must punish every sin—and He did, at the cross,

in the literal body of Jesus Christ. Here both justice and mercy met
and climaxed. God's justice, His righteous indignation against sin,
was satisfied, but it was satisfied in the person of Jesus Christ rather
than in the person of sinners themselves (that's the mercy part).

This is the key theme of Isaiah 53—vicarious atonement. All
through this chapter, these verses clearly and explicitly teach the idea
of the Suffering Servant taking the sin of others. This theme is also
the heart of New Testament theology. Christ died as a "sacrifice for
sins" (Hebrews 10:12). He "gave himself for our sins" (Galatians
1:14). He was "put to death for our trespasses" (Romans 4:25). Christ
"died for our sins once and for all" (1 Peter 3:18). "Christ died for
our sins in accordance with the Scriptures" (1 Corinthians 15:3). Christ
"died for the ungodly" (Romans 5:6). He "gave his life as a ransom
for many" (Matthew 10:28). This great truth was prefigured more
than seven centuries earlier in Isaiah 53.

Yet it doesn't end there, and that's what's touched on in verse 11.
Besides the overwhelming emphasis on the substitution, of the Suffering Servant taking upon Himself the penalty for our sins, the verse
"my Righteous Servant will justify many" implies what is made
explicit in the Pauline epistles—this Righteous Servant credits His
righteousness to those for whom He died. In other words, not only
does He take the penalty of the sinner's sins, but He can justify them,
or declare them righteous, because He alone among humanity has
the righteousness to give them in order that they may be righteous as
well. "For he [God] hath made him [Jesus] to be sin for us, who
knew no sin; that we might be made the righteousness of God in him"
(2 Corinthians 5:21).

Righteousness is linked to salvation because righteousness is the
foundation of salvation. "The Lord has made known *His salvation*; He
has revealed before the nations *His righteousness*" (Psalm 98:2, italics
supplied).[5] What makes the gospel unique is its teaching that righteous
works can never make a person righteous; only the righteousness of Christ,
credited or imputed to a person, can do that. Unlike other religions, where

the perfection, the holiness, or the righteousness needed to be saved is something to strive for, the gospel teaches that this perfection, holiness, and righteousness is where one begins. A Christian doesn't end the journey by finally attaining the righteousness of God; he starts out with it! This righteousness is the motive, not the goal, of a holy life, because by the very nature of things, humanity can never achieve it. To be righteous in the sight of God is to be *declared* righteous, and the only way to be declared righteous is to claim by faith the perfect righteousness wrought out by God's "Righteous Servant," Jesus Christ.

I am not ashamed of the gospel of Christ: for it is the power of God unto salvation to every one that believeth; to the Jew first, and also to the Greek. For therein is the righteousness of God revealed from faith to faith: as it is written, The just shall live by faith (Romans 1:16,17).

But now *the righteousness of God without the law is manifested,* being witnessed by the law and the prophets; Even *the righteousness of God which is by faith of Jesus Christ* unto all and upon all them that believe (Romans 3:21, 22, italics supplied).

I do not frustrate the grace of God: for if *righteousness come* by the law, then Christ is dead in vain (Galatians 2:21, italics supplied).

Even as Abraham believed God, and it was accounted to him for *righteousness* (Galatians 3:6, italics supplied).

Is the law then against the promises of God? God forbid: for if there had been a law given which could have given life, verily *righteousness* should have been by the law. But the scripture hath concluded all under sin, that the promise by faith of Jesus

Christ might be given to them that believe (Galatians 3:21, 22, italics supplied).

And be found in him, not having mine own *righteousness,* which is of the law, but that which is through the faith of Christ, the *righteousness* which is of God by faith (Philippians 3:9, italics supplied).

In short, Christ took our sin and iniquity and replaced it with His righteousness, "the righteousness which is of God by faith" Philippians 3:9). This is why Isaiah so often linked righteousness to salvation, because righteousness is the essence of salvation. There is no salvation apart from righteousness—and righteousness, like salvation, is something that God alone can provide. This righteousness is never anything that we can attain, in the sense of being made righteous enough to be saved (this is not the same as obedience, character perfection, or other aspects of what Scripture [James 3:18; Philippians 1:11; Hebrews 12:11] calls "the fruit of righteousness")— because then it would become a matter of salvation by works, and if salvation is of works, then it's no longer by faith. The righteousness that saves us, the righteousness that is so often paralleled to salvation in Isaiah, is the righteousness of God Himself, without a taint of human weaving woven in.

"For the Son of God," wrote John Calvin, "though spotlessly pure, took upon him the disgrace and ignominy of our iniquities, and in return clothed us with his purity."[6]

This is why we should have so much hope, so much reason to rejoice and have assurance of salvation. "Christ is become of no effect unto you, whosoever of you are justified by the law; ye are fallen from grace. For we through the Spirit wait for the *hope of righteousness* by faith" (Galatians 5:4, 5, italics supplied). And the reason for that hope of righteousness is that the righteousness we hope in, the righteousness at the core of our salvation, the righteousness which is by faith, is a righteousness that has already been worked out and acquired by Jesus Christ and which is then credited to us, apart from anything that we can do to earn it. The fact is we *can't* earn it. No matter how hard we try, no matter how holy we live, no matter how diligently we seek to obey God's law, *no matter how much "fruit of righteousness" we manifest in our own works and character,* we can no more reach this righteousness than we can reach to the heights of God by building a tower or by launching a rocket—because this righteousness is a perfect, holy righteousness, the righteousness of God Himself. If we get it, it's only because it has been given to us through the grace that comes by faith. "For by grace are ye saved through faith; and that not of yourselves: it is the gift of God" (Ephesians 2:8).

The gospel, then, at its core, is about the utter helplessness of mankind, the utter futility of his attempt to attain the most important goal in his existence—salvation. If that message isn't clear after six thousand years of wretched human history ("History is a nightmare" said James Joyce's Stephen Dedalus, "from which I am trying to awake")[7], then it never will be, especially if it hasn't become apparent in the last two thousand years, after the death of the Son of God Himself on the cross. If any possibility existed that we could save ourselves, Christ wouldn't have had to die. The fact that He died shows that we cannot save ourselves.

Salvation by works is, in fact, just another manifestation of the original sin: man trying to be God, in this case trying to do for himself that which only God can do for him. It's the height of pride when we take the prerogatives of God and try to make them our own. This is what led to the fall of Adam and what will lead to the final destruction of much of his seed. It's the ultimate folly, this working-your-way-to-heaven thing, a folly that love allowed and that only love could cure.

If the desire to be like God is at the foundation of all sin, then the prerequisite to being saved from sin is the opposite—a person has to understand his own utter inability to save himself, his own utter helplessness, his own utter sinfulness and depravity and unlikeness to

God. Sin began with an attitude; redemption does as well. If the attitude of wanting to be like God led to sin, then an attitude of knowing
just how unlike God we are leads to salvation. If pride led to death,
then humility leads to life. Salvation isn't unconditional; sinful, self-
centered man must respond to the Holy Spirit and make a conscious
choice to die to self. That's why Christians need to be broken, why
they need to take up their cross daily, and why Jesus said, "For whosoever will save his life shall lose it and whosoever will lose his life
for my sake shall find it" (Matthew 16:25). The attitude of total surrender, of sheer humility, of understanding our helplessness, of lean-
ing only on the merits of Christ as our only hope, moves a person as
far away as possible from the original sin, which was essentially an
attitude problem. Salvation starts with an "attitude adjustment." It's
what a person has to experience in order to be set on the narrow road
that leads to eternal life.

"The sacrifices of God are a broken spirit; a broken and crushed
spirit, O God, thou wilt not despise" (Psalm 51:17). And whose
heart can't be broken and crushed after glimpsing what Christ did
for us at the cross, all so powerfully depicted in Isaiah 53, where
verse after verse lobs on our souls the truth about Jesus taking the
punishment and penalty of our sins upon Himself? The chapter
depicts a reality that goes far beyond what people can fully com-
prehend; our four pound blobs of brain can no more understand
the full implications of the Cross than one can do differential cal-
culus on an abacus. Nothing in nature, nothing in history, nothing
in human consciousness pointed to the death of God on behalf of
sinners. It's totally the supernatural act of God. The Cross reveals
that truth extends far beyond what human experience and knowledge, in and of themselves, could ever render. Perhaps that's why
it has to be grasped by faith; reason and experience don't provide
enough grist for us to understand the reality that the Creator of
the universe would die for a small part of His creation. It's a truth
that has become especially problematic for modern man, whose

mind is limited by the constraints of untrammeled reason and the *a priori* materialistic presuppositions of science.

"In an era so unprecedently illuminated by science and reason," wrote Richard Tarnas, "the 'good news' of Christianity became less and less a convincing metaphysical structure, less secure a foundation upon which to build one's life, and less psychologically necessary. The sheer improbability of the whole nexus of events was becoming painfully obvious—that an infinite, eternal God would have suddenly become a particular human being in a specific historical time and place only to be ignominiously executed. That a single brief life taking place two millennia earlier in an obscure primitive nation, on a planet now known to be a relatively insignificant piece of matter revolving about one star among billions in an inconceivably vast and impersonal universe—that such an undistinguished event should have any overwhelming cosmic or eternal meaning could no longer be a compelling belief for reasonable men."[8]

And that's because the gospel represents a love that goes beyond reason. If sinful, erring, human love can take humans into realms that transcend reason, how much more the perfect love of God? It's so far beyond us that only through the "Spirit of truth" itself can we begin to grasp it.

Even the Spirit of truth; whom the world cannot receive, because it seeth him not, neither knoweth him: but ye know him; for he dwelleth with you, and shall be in you (John 14:17).

But when the Comforter is come, whom I will send unto you from the Father, even the Spirit of truth, which proceedeth from the Father, he shall testify of me (John 15:26).

Howbeit when he, the Spirit of truth, is come, he will guide you into all truth: for he shall not speak of himself; but whatso-

ever he shall hear, that shall he speak: and he will shew you
things to come (John 16:13).

We are of God: he that knoweth God heareth us; he that is
not of God heareth not us. Hereby know we the spirit of truth,
and the spirit of error (1 John 4:6).

No wonder, time and time again the New Testament talks about
hope—because the hope is not in ourselves; it's in God. Hope not
only in what He will do but hope in what He has already done
through Jesus, "by whom also we have access by faith into this
grace wherein we stand, and rejoice in hope of the glory of God.
And not only so, but we glory in tribulations also: knowing that
tribulation worketh patience; And patience, experience; and experience, hope: And hope maketh not ashamed; because the love
of God is shed abroad in our hearts by the Holy Ghost which is
given unto us. For when we were yet without strength, in due time
Christ died for the ungodly" (Romans 5:2-6). He died for the ungodly because the ungodly couldn't die for themselves. That's the
essence of love.

"God is love." Whatever that means, it means at least that love is
the transcendent metaphysic, the ultimate reality in which all else is
explained and apart from which nothing can be explained. Yet there's
a dichotomy in love: it's the reason we're in this mess—and the reason we're saved from it as well.

[1]St. Augustine, *The City of God* (New York: Image Books, 1958), 109.
[2]Aristotle, *Metaphysics* (*The Complete Works of Aristotle,*) Jonathan Barnes, ed. (Princeton/
Bollingen Series LXXI, 1958), 2:1554.
[3]Stephen Jay Gould, *Questioning the Millennium* (New York: Harmony Books, 1997), 16.
[4]*Early Writings,* 40.
[5]The vast majority of times in which "salvation" and "righteousness" appear in the same
verse occurs in Isaiah, although there are a few other places, such as Psalms, where the

parallel also appears: (Psalm 40:10; 24:5; 51:14; 119:123). This parallel can also be found in Romans 10:10—"For with the heart man believeth unto righteousness; and with the mouth confession is made unto salvation."

[6]John Calvin, *Institutes of the Christian Religion,* Henry Beveridge, trans. (Grand Rapids: Wm. B. Eerdmans Publishing Company, 1957), II, xvi, 6.

[7]James Joyce, *Ulysses* (New York: Vantage International, 1961), 34.

[8]Richard Tarnas, *The Passion of the Western Mind* (New York: Ballantine Books, 1991), 305.

# EIGHT

# The Old Law Tables

*" 'You shall not steal! You shall not kill!'—such words were once called holy; in their presence people bowed their knees and their heads and removed their shoes. But I ask you: Where have there been better thieves and killers in the world other than where such holy words have been? Is there not in all life itself— stealing and killing? And when such words were called holy was not truth itself—killed? Or was it a sermon of death that called holy that which contradicted and opposed all life?—O my brothers, shatter, shatter the old law tables."*
*—Friedrich Nietzche[1]*

About five centuries before Christ, in a debate with Socrates regarding morality, Glaucon argued that if no chance existed of being caught, a just man would act in the same way as an unjust one. "We shall catch the just man red-handed," Glaucon said, "in exactly the same pursuits as the unjust, led on by self-interest, the motive which all men naturally follow if they are not forcibly restrained by the law and made to respect each other's claims."[2]

To emphasize his point, Glaucon told the story of Gyges, a farmer who was herding his flock when an earthquake opened up the ground and revealed a bronze horse, hollow and fitted with doors. Gyges looked inside and saw a corpse with a gold ring on its finger. Gyges grabbed the ring and left. While sitting in the palace to pay his taxes, Gyges noticed that if he turned the ring inward, he became invisible; when he turned it back, he became visible again. Once he realized the great power in this ring, enabling him to do what he wanted without detection, how did Gyges respond? He seduced the queen, murdered the king, and seized the throne. According to Glaucon, if two rings existed, one for the just man, one for the unjust, neither "would have such iron strength of will as to stick to what is right and to keep his hands from taking other people's property."[3]

However negative, Glaucon's view of human nature rings uncomfortably true. How many people are "good" only because fear of social ostracism or punishment for breaking the law keeps them from being "evil"? Some, who might never shoplift, would step through that broken plate glass with contraband in their hands after the lights go out citywide. Considering all the crime committed even with the law in place, imagine what crimes would be committed without it.

Of course, technically, how can there be crime without law? For a crime to be committed, a law has to be broken. Crime, by its very definition, implies law.

It's the same with sin. If, as Scripture says, "sin is the transgression of the law" (1 John 3:4), then sin implies law. Sin can't exist without law, any more than crime can. As Paul said, "By the law is the knowledge of sin" (Romans 3:20). One can't talk about sin, in any meaningful manner, apart from law. "I had not known sin, but by the law: for I had not known lust, except the law had said, Thou shalt not covet" (Romans 7:7). Law might be able to exist without sin, as in heaven before Lucifer's folly,[4] but never vice versa.

How ironic, then, that many Christians who rail with vehemence against sin are reticent about championing law. Sin is sin only because God's law is God's law. To downplay the law is to downplay sin; to change the law is to change sin; to abolish the law is to abolish sin. One can't be altered without altering the other. To tamper with law is to move the goal posts in the middle of the game. If sin is defined in terms of law, then to manipulate the law is to manipulate sin, to blur the issue of good and evil—and that's a dangerous line to fuzz. "Woe to those who call evil good and good evil, who set darkness for light and light for darkness, who put bitter for sweet and sweet for bitter" (Isaiah 5:20).

Whether or not one admits it, as soon as one acknowledges the reality of sin, one acknowledges the reality of God's law. The law is as real as sin; in fact, the law predates sin, defines it, and gives it its existence. Because sin exists and permeates so much, if not all, of human existence, then God's law must exist and apply to all as well. If adultery is adultery in Moorish Spain, then it's adultery in Congregationalist Massachusetts, Vichy France, and on the moons of Jupiter. And it's adultery only because God's law defines it as such.

What's criminal in one nation might be legal in another, because human laws are based on tradition, culture, and politics. God's law, however, transcends tradition, culture, and politics. God's law always exists, everywhere with the same force, and it never changes. (How God deals with those who violate the law will differ from place to place, but that doesn't mean the law itself has changed[5]). What might not be criminal could still be sinful. God's law remains the same; man's reaction to it is the dynamic behind the law's interaction with humanity.

"The real problem," wrote Reinhold Neibuhr, "is presented by the prophetic recognition that all history is involved in a perennial defiance of the law of God."[6]

And because of defiance of this law, mankind needs a Savior. Sin, therefore, necessitated the gospel; if there were no sin, there would be no gospel because there would have been no need for it. The "good news" is that we can be saved despite having sinned. But we couldn't have sinned without law, thus it makes no sense to talk about the gospel apart from the law. They are of existential necessity related, even inseparable. Only in the context of the law can we understand the gospel. To preach the gospel without the law is to seek a cure without knowing the disease. How can a doctor prescribe a remedy without first understanding what's wrong with the patient? How can anyone preach the gospel without first knowing the law?

"The two can never be separated . . . " wrote Dietrich Bonhoeffer. "There can be no preaching of the law without the gospel, and no preaching of the gospel without the law . . . Whatever the Church's word to the world may be, it must always be *both* law *and* gospel."[7]

"The law and the gospel," wrote Ellen White, "go hand in hand. The one is the complement of the other. The law without faith in the gospel of Christ cannot save the transgressor of law. The gospel without the law is inefficient and powerless. The law and the gospel are a perfect whole. The Lord Jesus laid the foundation of the building, and He lays the headstone thereof with shoutings, crying, 'Grace, grace unto it' (Zech. 4:7). He is the author and finisher of our faith, the Alpha and Omega, the beginning and the end, the first and the last. The two blended—the gospel of Christ and the law of God— produce the love and faith unfeigned."[8]

Maybe for this reason, the book of Isaiah, though permeated with the gospel, with salvation, with God's righteousness, is also permeated with the law or, more specifically, with obedience. From beginning to end, "the gospel prophet" is as adamant about obedience as he is about forgiveness because the gospel, however much founded upon forgiveness and grace, can never be separated from obedience. Far from negating the law, or obedience, the gospel puts them in their proper perspective. The fact that the law can't save us, or that obedience can't be the ground of our justification, doesn't mean that the law isn't crucial or obedience mandatory. Scripture places salvation and obedience in harmony with each other and in an essential unity—not in tension much less contradiction with each other. Each helps define the other, and only together, in reference to one another, can the gospel and the law be really understood.

Law and gospel are like the subject and predicate of what Kant calls an analytic statement ("a rainy day is a watery day"). The gospel, by its very nature, implies law, just as a rainy day, by its very nature, implies water. A gospel that emphasizes forgiveness apart from the law is not the gospel of Jesus, Paul, or Isaiah. It's not the gospel at all. Isaiah proves this point if for no other reason than his repeated emphasis, even amid the gospel motif, on obedience, sin, and the law of God.

> Hear the word of the Lord, you rulers of Sodom; give ear to the *law of our God,* people of Gomorrah (Isaiah 1:10, italics supplied).

> Come, let us contend together, says the Lord. If your *sins* are as scarlet, they will be made white as snow, and if they are red like crimson they will be as wool. If you are willing and *will obey,* you will eat of the goodness of the land. But if you refuse and rebel, a sword will consume you, for the mouth of the Lord has spoken (Isaiah 1:18-20, italics supplied).

> Woe to those who draw iniquity with cords of vanity, and sins like the cords of a wagon (Isaiah 5:18).

> Therefore as fire consumes the stubble, and flames diminish the chaff, so shall their roots be as rottenness, and their buds as dust will go up, because they have rejected the *law of the Lord* of hosts and despised the word of the Holy One of Israel (Isaiah 5:24, italics supplied).

> For this is a rebellious people, lying children, children who do not want to hear *God's law* (Isaiah 30:9, italics supplied).

> The Lord is pleased for His righteousness' sake. He will magnify *the law* and make it honorable (Isaiah 42:21, italics supplied).

Who gave Jacob for spoil, and Israel for plunder? Was it not the Lord against whom we have sinned? For *we didn't want to* walk in His ways and we did not *obey His law* (Isaiah 42:24, italics supplied).

Let the wicked forsake his ways and the man of iniquity his thoughts (Isaiah 55:7).

Listen to me, my people, and give ear to me, my nation, because *a law* from me will go forth, and I will make rest my judgment as a light to the people (Isaiah 51:4, italics supplied).

I have spread all day my hands to a rebellious people who walk in a way not good, after their own thoughts (Isaiah 65:2).

Many more verses like these run through Isaiah. Even for Isaiah, who so eloquently presents the gospel, the importance of obedience to God's law rings apparent. If because of the gospel the law becomes optional, then obedience, even sin, suddenly becomes optional as well, and who believes that? The gospel doesn't void the law; it only strips the law of its power to destroy those who have violated it, because when we accept Christ by faith, we are then covered with Christ's righteousness, a righteousness wrought out in a life that perfectly kept the law. That's why the law couldn't hurt Christ. He never violated it, so it had no power to condemn Him, as it does us, who have violated it. And Christ's perfect standing, in relation to the law, is what He grants to those who claim Him by faith.

"Do we then make void the law through faith? God forbid: yea, we establish the law" (Romans 3:31).

How do we establish law? In the sense that the law, which leads us to Christ and the gospel, shows us more than ever our need of grace, because only through faith in Christ can we be saved. The law constantly keeps before us the need for grace.

To be saved from the legal consequences of sin doesn't mean that sin is now allowed, any more than being pardoned for a crime means you're now set free to continue committing that same crime. "Our faith in Christ," wrote Luther, "does not free us from works but from false opinions concerning works . . . the foolish presumption that justification is acquired by works."[9] Considering that sin brought the fall of Lucifer in heaven, the fall of man on earth, and the death of Christ on the cross, not to mention all the woes, suffering, and pain that every human being faces—then whatever the gospel means, it certainly doesn't mean that we're now free to continue in the very thing that has wrought so much damage to us. "What shall we say then? Shall we continue in sin, that grace may abound? God forbid!" (Romans 6:1, 2).

For the repenting and confessing Christian, the legal consequences of his sin have been paid, however the continued *dominion* of sin in our lives can still lead to destruction, because it's the devil's means of separating a person from the saving grace of Christ. We don't believe in once saved always saved. In the parable of the sower (Matthew 13), in Christ's words about blotting names out of the book of life (Revelation 3:5), in Paul's warning about the natural branches being broken off because of unbelief (Romans 11), the Bible is clear that born-again Christians can be lost—and the easiest way for this loss to occur is through sin that continues to *dominate* our lives.

This isn't the same as having a sinful nature; we all do, and always will, have a corrupted nature, at least until the second coming of Christ. Nor is this the same as struggling with certain inherited or cultivated weaknesses; we all have aspects in our lives that are harder to control or have victory over than others. This isn't the same as dealing with defects in character; we are all born defective, of defective parents in a defective world with defective influences all around us. And most of all, this isn't the painful awareness of our unworthiness and unrighteousness before God.

Instead, this is about when sin *dominates*; when we serve sin;

when sin is the controlling factor in our lives; when we constantly choose sin over Christ. Then we have a problem—not a hopeless problem to be sure, not one that God hasn't done everything possible to remedy, not one that can't be fixed—but a problem nonetheless. Not because God can't forgive the sin that dominates our lives (the provision for its forgiveness was already accomplished at the cross), but because sooner or later that sin will so push us away from the Lord that we'll no longer see a need to truly repent of that sin, much less forsake it.

What Christian hasn't experienced what sin does to his or her relationship with Christ? Who hasn't felt the power of sin to bring about such guilt that we fear we're lost or that we're too degenerate to be saved? Who has never heard Satan's whispers that we're just not good enough, that God will never forgive our sins, especially the ones that we commit over and over?

The crucial question is, When do Christians experience this separation, guilt, and hopelessness? When, through the grace and power of God, they claim His promises of power to resist temptation and get victory? Or when, not choosing to surrender to Christ, not choosing to suffer in the flesh ("for he that hath suffered in the flesh hath ceased from sin" 1 Peter 4:1), they allow themselves to be betrayed into sin?

It's the latter, of course. How many feel overwhelming guilt or despair of salvation when, through the grace of Christ, they withstand the clamors of the flesh? That's not the paradigm. Instead, doubt, guilt, despair, and separation often reign when people fall into sin, when they let go of God's promises (or never even claim them), and succumb to temptation. This is when they give up, when Satan uses their sin to separate them from Christ.

"Behold, the hand of the Lord is not too short to save, and His ears are not too heavy to hear; but your iniquities have separated you from your God" (Isaiah 59:1, 2).

Bemoaning our sinfulness before God isn't the same as serving sin so that it separates us from a saving relationship with Him. One acknowledges the reality of sin in our character and draws us to the cross; the other allows sin to so consume us that we run from the cross. One makes us realize our need of the gospel; the other can neutralize all the power of the gospel in our lives. How ironic that sin, the one thing that makes us need the cross, can be the one thing that Satan uses to make us flee it.

Victory over sin, or obedience to God's law, isn't a prerequisite for salvation. It's too late for the law to do anything other than condemn. The law might show us what we need to do, but it never can give us the power to do it. Overcoming sin can never be the foundation of salvation; salvation must always be by grace through faith alone.

"There is not a point," wrote Ellen White, "that needs to be dwelt upon more earnestly, repeated more frequently, or established more firmly in the minds of all than the impossibility of fallen man meriting anything by his own best good works. Salvation is through faith in Jesus Christ alone."[10]

But obedience to God, to His law, as we serve "in newness of spirit, and not in the oldness of the letter" (Romans 7:6) is the personal manifestation of that salvation in the life of the Christian. Just as obedience doesn't save us, neither does more obedience make us "more" saved. Growing in grace doesn't mean we are any more saved than before; growing in grace can mean, instead, that we're more secure in that salvation, walking closer to the Lord, manifesting more of the character of Christ in our lives, and also being more aware of right and wrong. "But strong meat belongeth to them that are of full age, even those who by reason of use have their senses exercised to discern both good and evil" (Hebrews 5:14).

This last point is crucial. Sin—even confessed, forgiven, and repented of—damages the sinner. How many people's lives have been ruined, or made exceedingly difficult, by sins that have been covered by Christ's blood? David's murder, adultery, coveting, and lying were forgiven the instant he confessed; the effects remained long after.

And one of the most dangerous effects of sin, forgiven or otherwise, is that it desensitizes the sinner to the evil of the sin itself. Christ's death has provided the means through which we can be forgiven the same sin, over and over and over (anyone dare to venture a cut-off number?). But the act of committing that same sin over and over will deaden our abhorrence of its sinfulness. Who hasn't, because of something or other repeatedly done, found himself resigned to, or even justifying, what he once found repulsive?

This effect can be seen in the world, not just in Christians. It's a principle; it's how our brains are wired. A few years ago in Texas, for example, six public high school teachers were suspended without pay for using in class a math worksheet containing the following questions:

Johnny has an AK-47 with an eighty-round clip. If he misses six out of ten shots and shoots thirteen times during each drive-by shooting, how many drive-by shootings can he attempt before he has to reload?

Jose has two ounces of cocaine. He sells an eight-ball to Jackson for $320 and two grams to Billy for $85 per gram. What is the street value of the balance of cocaine if he doesn't cut it?

Rufus is pimping for three girls. If the price is $65 for each trick, how many tricks will each girl have to turn so that Rufus can pay for his $800-per-day crack habit.[11]

Would questions like these have been put on a high school exam ten, fifteen, or twenty years ago? Of course not. We've just become acclimatized to evil. *Harper's Magazine* editor Lewis H. Lapham—commenting on the dark days when Hollywood movies were censored, when dirty novels were banned, and when "sex was something that happened in France"—wrote that the changes in American society from those days "probably have been for the better." In the same article, however, he writes: "Over the years I've listened to a good many stories of bewilderment and loss, but none sadder than the one that appeared in the tabloids on June 9 about an eighteen-year-old girl, a student at the Lacy Township School in Ocean County, New Jersey, to whom a son was born at her graduation prom. During the break in the music, she left the ballroom, gave birth to the baby in the bathroom stall, wrapped it in paper towels, discarded it in a wastebasket, washed her hands, smoothed her evening dress, and returned for the next dance."[12] What Lapham doesn't seem to understand is that the story he finds so sad results directly from the moral changes that he thinks "probably have been for the better."

Lepers who lose their fingers and toes don't lose them as a direct result of the disease; they lose them because their nerves have been so damaged by the disease that they can't feel burns or sharp objects, and thus they don't immediately remove their fingers or toes upon contact. Sin, even forgiven sin, does the same. "To violate one's conscience," wrote Graham Maxwell, "is to weaken the ability to discern between right and wrong."[13]

"Conscience! Conscience! Divine instinct, immortal voice from heaven," wrote French romantic Jean Jacques Rousseau. "Immortal guide for a creature ignorant and finite indeed; yet intelligent and free; infallible judge of good and evil, making man like to God ['You shall be like God']! In thee consists the excellence of man's nature and the morality of his actions."[14]

Conscience, however, is constantly hardened by violations, and nothing turns our brains into cement more than sin. Who repents of, confesses, or forsakes what his conscience no longer tells him is sinful? Sin is a deception, and Christians who are dominated by sin are dominated by a deception that opens them up to abandoning their saving relationship with Christ, whether they know it or not. "But exhort one another daily, while it is called Today; lest any of you be hardened through the deceitfulness of sin" (Hebrews 3:13). This is exactly what happened to Judas; none of us are immune either.[15]

"Woe to those who call evil good and good evil, who put darkness for light and light for darkness, who put bitter for sweet and sweet for bitter" (Isaiah 5:20).

Sin can so deceive us that the distinction between evil and good not only becomes blurred but reversed until, as Isaiah wrote, people call good evil and evil good, darkness light and light darkness, and bitter sweet and sweet bitter. And who's going to repent of the dark, bitter, and evil that appears as light, sweet, and good?

That sins can be forgiven is a given; the cross took care of that problem once and for all. But whether we will continue to always seek this forgiveness over and over again for sins that dominate our lives? . . . that becomes problematic. "Every sinful gratification," wrote Ellen White, "tends to benumb the faculties and deaden the mental and spiritual perceptions, and the word or the Spirit of God can make but a feeble impression upon the heart."[16]

No wonder that Isaiah, the *gospel* prophet, has such strong words about sin, about iniquity, and rebellion and why he stressed obedience to the law so much. In the midst of the good news about justification, of Christ's atoning death, of His substitution, he nevertheless writes:

Woe, *sinful* nation, a people heavy with *iniquity*, the seed of evildoers, corrupted children; they have forsaken the Lord, they have despised the Holy One of Israel; they have gone backward (Isaiah 1:4, italics supplied).

Woe to the *rebellious* children, says the Lord, who take counsel but not from me, who pour out offerings but not according to my Spirit, in order that they may add sin to sin" (Isaiah 30:1, italics supplied).

The righteous perish and no man considered it; the merciful are taken away, and none understand that from before the evil the righteous are taken away. . . . But you, come near, sons of the barbarian and seed of the *adulterer and whore.* Against whom do you make merry over, against whom do you widen your mouth and stick out your tongue. Are you not the children of *transgressors,* the seed of a *lie,* burning yourselves with idols under every green tree and destroying children in the valleys under the clefts of the rocks? (Isaiah 57: 1, 3-6, italics supplied).

For your hands are with blood, and your fingers with *iniquity;* your lips have spoken lies, your tongue has uttered injustice. None calls for righteousness, and none judges for truth, and they trust in vanity, they speak lies, they conceive trouble, and give birth to *iniquity* . . . their works are works of iniquity, and violent deeds are in their hands. Their feet run toward evil, and they hurry to pour out innocent blood, their thoughts are thoughts of iniquity, destruction and violence are in their paths (Isaiah 59:3, 4, 6, 7, italics supplied).

None of these verses make sense apart from the law. They implicitly prove the existence of God's law, because without it there could be none of the sin, iniquity, and transgression that Isaiah rails against. "To the law and to the testimony; if they speak not according to this word, there is no light in them" (Isaiah 8:20).

Nevertheless, as Paul could write centuries later, "But where sin abounded, grace did much more abound" (Romans 5:20). Here's the wonderment of truth so prevalent in Isaiah—amid the scathing rebukes against sin, rebellion, and iniquity, salvation in Christ rings out. Interwoven with all the warnings, threats, and admonitions to obey—in fact, because of them—Isaiah radiates with wonderful promises of the hope of redemption in the Messiah, because that's the only answer for sin and disobedience.

Sin might be able to exist without the gospel, but never vice versa.

The gospel and sin are explicitly mingled because the only cure for sin *is* the gospel. Why would the Lord rail against evil if nothing could be done about it? And the only thing that can be done about it is what Christ has done. "It will be seen," wrote Ellen White, "that He who is infinite in wisdom could devise no plan for our salvation except the sacrifice of His Son."[17] That's why Isaiah is so full of Christ.

Therefore, the Lord, He will give to you a sign: Behold a virgin shall conceive, and she will give birth to a son, and you will call His name Immanuel (Isaiah 7:14).

For a child is born to us, a son is given to us, and dominion will be upon His shoulder; and his name shall be called, Wonderful, Counselor, the Mighty God, Eternal Father, Prince of Peace (Isaiah 9:6).

And a rod will come forth from the stock of Jesse, and a branch from his roots will bear fruit. And the Spirit of the Lord shall rest upon Him, the Spirit of wisdom and insight, the Spirit of counsel and might, the Spirit of knowledge and fear of the Lord (Isaiah 11:1, 2).

Therefore, thus says the Lord God, "Behold, I lay a foundation in Zion, a stone, a test stone, a precious cornerstone, a sure foundation" (Isaiah 28:16).

Behold, I have engraved you on the palms of my hands (Isaiah 49:16).

Surely He has carried our infirmities and borne our sufferings. . . . And he was profaned from our transgressions and He was crushed from our iniquities, and the punishment of our peace was upon Him . . . and the Lord has put on Him the iniquity of all of

us . . . because of the transgression of my people He was smitten. . . . You shall make His life an offering for sin . . . with His
knowledge will My Righteous Servant justify many; and their
iniquities He will bear. . . . He carried the sins of many and made
intercession for the transgressors (Isaiah 53:4-12).

The Spirit of the Lord God is upon me, because the Lord
anointed Me to preach the good news to the afflicted; He sent
me to bind up the brokenhearted, to proclaim liberty to the captives, and an open hope to those who are bound; to proclaim the
acceptable year of the Lord, the day of vengeance of our God,
and to comfort all that mourn (Isaiah 61:1, 2).

Whatever the specific historical and political situation in Isaiah,
the problem of sin is universal; whatever the specific and primary
applications of the Messianic prophecies, Christ's atonement is
universal as well. The cure is broad enough and powerful enough to
heal the disease, no matter how badly corrupted the body.

"Why should you still be stricken, and continue to revolt? The
whole head is sick, the whole heart faint. From the bottom of the foot
to the head, there is no soundness in it; sores, breaks, fresh boils that
are not closed up nor bound nor treated with oil" (Isaiah 1:5, 6).

Yet Isaiah gives also a wonderful promise to those who choose
God, who choose to turn away from sin, from rebellion, and to surrender their lives to God in obedience to His commandments:

Seek the Lord while He may be found; call upon Him in His
nearness. Let the wicked forsake his ways, and the man of iniquity his thoughts, and let him return unto the Lord and He will
have mercy upon him, and to his God, for He will greatly pardon. For my thoughts are not your thoughts, nor my ways your
ways, says the Lord. As the heavens are higher than the earth,
thus my ways are higher than your ways and my thoughts than

your thoughts. For as the rain and the snow come down from heaven and do not return there, but water the earth and make it bear and bud so that it gives seed to the sower and bread to the eater—my word, which goes forth from my mouth, will not return unto me vain but will do that which I delight and it will prosper in that which I sent it (Isaiah 55:6-11).

God's thoughts are not our thoughts, His ways are not our ways, because our thoughts could never have imagined the plan of salvation nor our ways consummated it. That we, as sinful, fallen beings, could not only be reconciled to the God against whom we have so boldly transgressed but also be cleansed from sin and live in obedience to God and His law is a thought that we could have never conceived ourselves (much less bring to fruition). Instead, it's one that had to be told us, and even then we internalize it only by faith because reason alone isn't efficacious enough or broad enough to contain it.

The beauty of the gospel is at once its transcendence and its immediacy; it's a reality conceived separate from humanity yet brought to fruition in humankind; it's a truth realized apart from human beings (for atonement is God's work only), yet expressed and experienced only in them. It's something that no human could have done and yet was done (in its immediate context) only for humans.

The good news of the gospel isn't just what happened at the first coming or what will happen at the second; it covers what happens in between because the same power—one greater than all the powers of humanity—that freed Christ from the bonds of the grave works to free us from the bondage of sin. "But if the Spirit of him that raised up Jesus from the dead dwell in you, he that raised up Christ from the dead shall also quicken your mortal bodies by his Spirit that dwelleth in you" (Romans 8:11).

Through Christ we have not just freedom from the condemnation of sin but from its dominance in our lives. God wouldn't call us to put away sin if the possibility of doing it didn't exist, and it exists because the supernatural power that dwells in us makes that possibility real.

Like Gyges, we have been given supernatural power. Unlike Gyges, who used this power to defy the law, we've been given it not only to bring us into harmony with the law but also to bring us into harmony with a standard of righteousness and holiness that far transcends the law—a righteousness and holiness that comes from the One who said: "The Spirit of the Lord God is upon me, because the Lord anointed me to preach the good news to the afflicted; He sent me to bind up the brokenhearted, to proclaim liberty to the captives, and an open hope to those who are bound; to proclaim the acceptable year of the Lord, the day of vengeance of our God, and to comfort all that mourn" (Isaiah 61:1, 2). "Look unto me and be saved, all the ends of the earth; for I am God and there is no other. I have sworn by myself: from my mouth a word has gone forth in righteousness and will not return to me, until every knee will bow and every tongue swear. Surely, one will say, 'In the Lord I have righteousness and strength . . . In the Lord all the seed of Israel will be justified and glorified' " (Isaiah 45:22-25).

---

[1]Friedrich Nietzsche, *Thus Spake Zarathustra* (New York: Penguin Books,1969), 219.
[2]Plato, *The Republic* (New York: Penguin Classics, 1987), 105.
[3]*Ibid.*, 106.
[4]"But in heaven, service is not rendered in the spirit of legality. When Satan rebelled against the law of Jehovah, the thought that there was a law came to the angels almost as an awakening to something unthought of. In their ministry the angels are not as servants, but as sons. There is perfect unity between them and their Creator. Obedience is to them no drudgery. Love for God makes their service a joy. So in every soul wherein Christ, the hope of glory, dwells, His words are reechoed, 'I delight to do Thy will, O My God: yea, Thy law is within My heart. Psalm 40:8.' " *Thoughts From the Mount of Blessing,* 109.

"Good angels wept to hear the words of Satan, and his exulting boasts. God declared that the rebellious should remain in Heaven no longer. Their high and happy state had been held upon condition of obedience to the law which God had given to govern the high order of intelligences. But no provision had been made to save those who should venture to transgress his law." *Spirit of Prophecy,* 1:22.

[5]Paul touches on this topic in Romans 2:11-16. "For there is no respect of persons with God. For as many as have sinned without law shall also perish without law: and as many as have sinned in the law shall be judged by the law; (For not the hearers of the law are just before God, but the doers of the law shall be justified. For when the Gentiles, which have not the law, do by nature the things contained in the law, these, having not the law, are a law unto themselves: which shew the work of the law written in their hearts, their conscience also bearing witness, and their thoughts the meanwhile accusing or else excusing one another;) in the day when God shall judge the secrets of men by Jesus Christ according to my gospel."

[6]Reinhold Niebuhr, *The Nature and Destiny of Man* (New York: Charles Scribner's Sons, 1964), 29.

[7]Dietrich Bonhoeffer, *Ethics* (New York: Macmillan Books, 1986), 357, 358.

[8]*Our High Calling,* 141.

[9]Martin Luther, *The Freedom of a Christian,* quoted in Garret Ward Sheldon, *Religion and Politics* (New York: Peter Lang, 1990), 67.

[10]*Faith and Works,* 19.

[11]"Lowest Common Denominator," *Harper's Magazine,* November 1997, 20.

[12]Lewis H. Lampan "In the Garden of Tabloid Delight," *Harper's Magazine,* August 1997, 38, 39.

[13]Graham Maxwell, *Servants or Friends?* (Redlands, Calif.: Pineknoll Publications, 1992), 104.

[14]Jean Jacques Rousseau, *Emile* (London: Everyman's Library, 1965), 254.

[15]See *The Desire of Ages,* 716-722.

[16]*The Great Controversy,* 474.

[17]*Ibid.,* 652.

# That Promise
# of Hell

### The Hand That Signed the Paper

*The hand that signed the paper felled a city*
*Five sovereign fingers taxed the breath,*
*Doubled the globe of dead and halved a country;*
*These five kings did a king to death.*

*The mighty  hand leads to a sloping shoulder*
*The finger joints are cramped with chalk*
*A goose's quill has put an end to murder*
*That put an end to talk.*

*The hand that signed the treaty bred a fever*
*And famine grew, and locusts came;*
*Great is the hand that holds dominion over*
*Man by a scribbled name.*

*The five kings count the dead but do not soften*
*The crusted wound nor stroke the brow;*
*A hand rules pity as a hand rules heaven;*
*Hands have no tears to flow.*
*—Dylan Thomas[1]*

The day he was to hang, the condemned man consumed peas, bread, olives, tea, a normal evening repast. At 8:00 p.m., he was informed that his plea for mercy, that his life be spared, that his death sentence be delayed, had been rejected. He would die, by midnight. A Christian missionary entered the cold cell and pleaded, "Repent!" The prisoner shrugged him off. When the Christian suggested that they read the Bible together, he uttered, "I don't have time to waste." With just a few hours left, he didn't.

A prison orderly brought him a bottle. Red wine. He drank half. As midnight approached he was led to the third floor gallows. When asked if he wanted to wear a black hood, the prisoner responded, "No!"

He was pronounced dead at 11:58 p.m. The body was cut down, then cremated, the ashes strewn over waves far out in the sea.

The date of the execution: May 31, 1962. The water that took the charred remains: the Mediterranean. The executioners: Jews. The executed: Nazi war criminal Adolph Eichmann.

Adolph Eichmann, a former oil company salesman, ran Hitler's "final solution." Millions of men, women, and children were ruthlessly and mercilessly murdered through the diligence of this icy German bureaucrat who constantly complained about obstacles in fulfilling death camp quotas or about the uncooperativeness of German allies in handing over their Hebrews. Once, when asked what should be done with 4,000 Jewish children isolated at a station, Eichmann replied that as soon as trains were available, "transports of children would be able to roll" and they should be sent to Auschwitz, where all were gassed, their little bodies stuffed en mass in ovens and burned.

But to hang a man who had killed millions in the same way you'd hang him if he had killed just one—how can that be justice? It can't be, nor was it. Eichmann deserved more punishment than what the Israelis gave or could ever give. Some things are beyond human potentiality to conceive, much less consummate. Who among us could devise a punishment equal to this crime? None of us could, which is why none of us do.

Only God can, and He will. It's called hell, and there's comfort in the promise of it.

Why? Because only in anticipation of the promise that justice will be done can I have any peace amid a world reeking with such outrageous offense. It's because I know that then, in the midst of that divine fire, all the evil that has gone unaccounted for and unpunished will finally be accounted for and punished. Only in hell will the final, total vindication of the character of God be consummated. There's been too much pain, too much injustice, too much cruelty, too much torture, too much brutality for too long for God not to punish it. If there were no hell, there would be no justice, and with no justice there could be no just God.

In fact, with just one premise—that if God is just, then logic demands divine retribution—Immanuel Kant once argued for the existence of an afterlife because, he said, if God is just, there had to be a final reckoning because there's no justice in this life. American patriot Ethan Allen in *Reason, the Only Oracle of Man,* arguing from the premise of God's justice, wrote, "Justice in all events does not take place in this world," therefore, "there must be an existence beyond this life, where the ultimate justice of God will take place."[2] And that's true, because justice doesn't, in fact can't, take place here.

How could it?

One account from World War II tells about a baby left out in the cold by the Nazis to die; the infant chewed its frozen numb fingers down to nothing but black nubs. Historian Max Dimont wrote that when the Jews resisted, the Germans didn't torture them, they tortured their children instead. "An infant would be torn in two by its legs in front of its parents; a child's head would be smashed against a tree and the bloody remains handed to the mother; a teenage girl would be raped and then impaled on a bayonet while her brothers and sisters were forced to watch."[3] Another eyewitness said that when "the extermination of the Jews in the gas chambers was at its height, orders were issued that children were to be thrown

straight into the crematorium furnaces, or into a pit near the crematorium, without being gassed first."[4] The Nazis used to celebrate the Day
of Atonement in Auschwitz by killing hundreds of extra children each
time the holiday rolled around. Non-Jewish Poles described what the
Germans did to inhabitants in the Warsaw ghetto:

> The prescribed number of victims is 8,000-10,000 daily. . . .
> Children cannot walk on their strength and are loaded into wag-
> ons. The process of loading is so brutal that very few survive it.
> Mothers, looking on, become insane. . . . Railroad cars wait on
> the ramp. The executioners pack the condemned into the wag-
> ons, 150 of them in one wagon. On the floors of the wagons lies
> a thick layer of lime and chloride poured over with water. The
> door of the wagon gets sealed. Sometimes the wagon moves
> immediately after loading, sometimes it stays on the side rails a
> day, two—it doesn't matter to anyone anymore. Of the people
> crammed so tightly that the dead cannot fall, but keep standing
> arm in arm with the living, of the people slowly dying in the
> fumes of the lime and chloride, being deprived of air, water,
> food—no one will remain alive anyway.[5]

One Nazi described a scene in which Russian Jews were stripped
and thrown into a pit before being shot. "Why did that scene linger so
long in my memory? Perhaps because I had children myself. And
there were children in that pit. I saw a woman holding a child of a
year or two in the air, pleading. At that moment all I wanted to say
was, 'Don't shoot, hand over the child.' Then the child was hit. I was
so close that later I found bits of brains splattered on my coat."[6]

The German telling the story: Adolph Eichmann.

Years ago, a Ukranian immigrant to the United States, John
Demjanjuk, was accused of being Ivan the Terrible, a guard at
Treblinka who used to torture the victims, especially women and
children. Ivan, often wielding a sword or bayonet, would herd people

into the chamber (which he would operate), often hacking off women's breasts or noses in the process. At times he would take elderly bearded men with sidelocks and place their heads between taut strands of barbed wire. As he beat them, they would writhe in pain and strangle themselves. During Demjanjuk's trial in Israel, one witness told of a girl of about twelve who had survived the gas chamber and was lying amid a pile of corpses, crying out for her mother. Ivan ordered a Jewish prisoner to rape her. When the man refused, Ivan shot them both.

Eventually, the Israelis determined that Demjanjuk wasn't Ivan the Terrible (though apparently he had been a guard at another camp) and let him go. Ivan, supposedly, had been killed by the Russians.

But suppose Demjanjuk had been guilty and executed? Would that have been justice? And if Ivan the Terrible was, indeed, killed by the Russians, does that pay for his crimes? Only twenty-two big-wig Nazis ever faced trial for their roles in the murder of millions, and of them only twelve were hung, some were given life sentences, others lesser terms, and two were acquitted. Justice? Meanwhile, how many tens of thousands of other brutal killers, the ones who raped the women and impaled them on bayonets, or who threw the screamimg children into the flames, have been punished? Many are living the good life in the U.S. or on nice pensions paid to them now by the German government for their service in the Second World War. And even if they were caught and punished, how can any human punishment equal these crimes?

Suppose that was my son or daughter thrown alive into the flames? Suppose they were yours? Does it matter whose they were? What punishment could sufficiently pay for one of their deaths, much less thousands? None can, at least none here. That's why there has to be a final reckoning. It's called hell, and it's where God's wrath against evil will be finally consummated.

A loving God is capable of anger; He'd have to be. In fact, His anger stems directly from His love. What makes a person more angry, seeing an evil and injustice done to someone they don't love or to someone they do? The latter, obviously. Thus, if God loves the world, how could He not have wrath and indignation on what sin has done to human beings, no matter how far beyond our understanding that wrath or that anger might be? If God loves the world, then He must be—among other things—angry at what has happened to it.

For me (and I'm purposely writing this chapter in first person singular because it's so personal), the Holocaust demands that if a just God exists, hell must too. If there were no hell, it would be better that there be no God, because it would be easier to accept the injustice and evil in a world without God than one with a God who allowed all these things but didn't bring final retribution for them. Given the cold reality of history, I couldn't love God if there were no promise of hell. In a world where injustice can leave even the most perceptive, incisive souls groping in the darkness of what appears so confusedly absurd and unfair, hell is the only thing that can make any sense of it all.

However difficult it is to accept the horrors of what human beings inflict upon one another, especially given the reality of a loving, powerful Creator, these atrocities can be made to fit into the overarching template of the great controversy between good and evil. The great controversy theme works, but only with the promise of divine retribution. Hell is the final, closing stage in the great drama between Christ and Satan. Without it, the controversy could never come to a satisfactory conclusion; there would be too many loose ends, too many unanswered questions, too many sins unaccounted for. In the final cleansing fire, all loose ends are neatly tied, all questions resolved, all sins accounted for. In hell, God's justice will be finally and fully consummated.

I'm not talking about the Catholic and Protestant nonsense of eternal torment, a doctrine that makes God worse than the Nazis. If hell is eternal, *then evil ultimately wins*, and the angel with the flaming sword meant to keep sinners from eating from the tree of life failed in his task. I'm not talking even about common notions of a presently burning hell, some hole in the earth where right now people are frying, a concept perhaps expressed best in contemporary terms by rocker Kurt Cobain in *Lake of Fire:*

> Where do bad folks go when they die
> They don't go to heaven where the angels fly.
> They go to a lake of fire and fry,
> And you won't see them again until the fourth of July.[7]

I'm talking, instead, about an infinitely loving God who has paid the full penalty for all our sins; a God who knows all hearts, motives, and actions; a God who will execute judgment in a perfect balance of mercy and justice. I'm talking about when the Lord will, as Jesus said, "reward every man according to his works" (Matthew 16:27), when God "will render to every man according to his deeds" (Romans 2:6). I'm talking about the God who said "Vengeance belongeth unto me, I will recompense, saith the Lord" (Hebrews 10:30). I'm talking about the consuming flames of hell, which is nothing but God giving those who have refused to accept what He's done for them the rewards of what they have done to themselves—and others. A just God couldn't do anything else.

Ellen White wrote:

> I saw the mercy and compassion of God in giving his Son to die for guilty man. Those who will not choose to accept salvation which has been so dearly purchased for them, must be punished. Beings whom God created have chosen to rebel against his government; but I saw that God did not shut them up in hell to endure endless misery. He could not take them to heaven; for to bring them into the company of the pure and holy would make them perfectly miserable. God will not take them to heaven, neither will he cause them to suffer eternally. He will destroy

them utterly, and cause them to be as though they had not been, and then his justice will be satisfied. He formed man out of the dust of the earth, and the disobedient and unholy will be consumed by fire, and return to dust again. I saw that the benevolence and compassion of God in this, should lead all to admire his character, and to adore him; and after the wicked shall be destroyed from off the earth, all the heavenly host will say, Amen![8]

The book of Isaiah, so richly filled with the love of God, with the hope of salvation in Jesus, is also so richly filled with powerful descriptions of God's justice. Isaiah is woven tight with warnings, promises, and depictions of God's ultimate judgment against evil. It's not a contradiction, nor a paradox, to place the forgiving love of God as revealed in Christ's first coming alongside His justice and judgment as revealed in His second coming (and beyond). According to Hebrew scholar Dr. Jacques Doukhan, love and justice are inseparable concepts in Scripture. "On God's level," he wrote, "the incredible act of the cross, the incarnation of the love of heaven, also appeals to the concept of justice. The same root, *sdq* [the root for "righteousness"], conveys both notions, which are disassociated in our languages. In the Bible it is inconceivable to separate love from justice; therefore the two are associated together. . . . Salvation had to be mixed with judgment. Salvation had to be achieved according to the criterion of justice."[9]

Isaiah reiterates the theme of God's justice. Whether or not the immediate context is the final punishment of sin in "the lake of fire" (Revelation 19:10; 20:10, 14, 15) or whether it's local events that symbolize cosmic ones or whether some verses have multiple fulfillments—the gospel prophet teaches that God will punish unredeemed evil.

Zion will be redeemed with judgment and her captives with righteousness. And the destruction of the rebellious and of sinners will be together, and those that forsake the Lord shall be consumed (Isaiah 1:27, 28).

Go into the rock, hide yourself in the dust from before the fear of the Lord, and from the glory of His majesty. And the exalted looks of man will be brought low, and the haughtiness of men will bow down, and the Lord alone will be exalted on that day. For the day of the Lord of Hosts will be upon all who are proud and exalted, and upon all who are lifted up. . . . And the loftiness of man will bow down and will be brought low, and the Lord alone will be exalted on that day. And He will utterly destroy the idols. And they will go into the holes of the rocks, and into the caves of dust from before the fear of the Lord and from the glory of His majesty, when He arises to break the earth. On that day a man will cast away his idols of silver and of gold, which he made for himself to worship, to the moles and to the bats, to go into the clefts of the rocks, and to the tops of the cliffs, from before the fear of the Lord and from the glory of His majesty, when He arises to break the earth (Isaiah 2:10-12; 17-21).

Behold, the day of the Lord comes, angry, with wrath and heat, to make the land desolate, and sinners He will destroy from upon it. For the stars of heaven and the constellations will not shine their light. The sun shall be darkened when it goes forth and the moon will not shine her light. And I will punish the world for its evil and the wicked for their iniquity, and I will stop the pride of the proud, and the arrogance of the mighty I will humble (Isaiah 13:9-11).

The world will greatly totter, like a drunk, and it will flutter like a hut, and the transgression will be heavy upon it, and it will fall and not rise again. And it will come to pass that on that day the Lord will punish the host of the exalted ones in their exaltation, and the kings of the land upon the land. And the prisoners will be gathered together, prisoners to a pit, and they will be shut up in prison, and after many days they will be punished (Isaiah 24:20-22).

Come, my people, enter into your chambers, and shut your doors behind yourself, as in a little moment, until the indignation be past. Behold, the Lord comes from His place to punish the iniquity of the inhabitants of the earth; and the earth will reveal her blood and not still cover her slain (Isaiah 26:20, 21).

For it will be the day of vengeance to the Lord, the year of recompense for the controversy of Zion. And its streams will be turned to pitch, and its dust to brimstone, and the land will be burning pitch. Neither by night nor day will it be quenched; its smoke will ascend forever; it will lie wasted from generation to generation. For ever and ever none will pass through it (Isaiah 34:8-10).

And he put on righteousness as a breastplate, and a helmet of salvation upon his head, and he will dress in garments of vengeance for clothing, and he was clad with zeal as a cloak. According to their works, accordingly, he will repay: fury to his adversaries, recompense to his enemies; to the isles he will repay recompense (Isaiah 59:17).

This is not just Old Testament imagery of an angry God. These truths are taught in the New Testament as well. In fact, the book of Revelation borrows concepts and imagery of divine retribution from Isaiah.

And said to the mountains and rocks, Fall on us, and hide us from the face of him that sitteth on the throne, and from the wrath of the Lamb (Revelation 6:16).

And the smoke of their torment ascendeth up for ever and ever: and they have no rest day nor night, who worship the beast and his image, and whosoever receiveth the mark of his name (Revelation 14:11).

And the beast was taken, and with him the false prophet that wrought miracles before him, with which he deceived them that had received the mark of the beast, and them that worshipped his image. These both were cast alive into a lake of fire burning with brimstone (Revelation 19:20).

And after these things I heard a great voice of much people in heaven, saying, Alleluia; Salvation, and glory, and honour, and power, unto the Lord our God: For true and righteous are his judgments: for he hath judged the great whore, which did corrupt the earth with her fornication, and hath avenged the blood of his servants at her hand (Revelation 19:1, 2).

There's no question: The Lord will execute justice at the end of the world. A just God, to be just, has to, because He certainly isn't executing it now due to the moral constraints He's placed on Himself in His divine plan to fully answer the question of evil. Some justice does happen in this life, but only partially. And a perfectly just God, by definition, must execute justice perfectly, not partly. The principle that a person reaps what he sows exists, but it is not fully manifested at present (Who's going to tell me that the baby who chewed its fingers down to black nubs or any one of those 4,000 children waiting for the train to take them to Auschwitz simply reaped what they had sown?). There are natural consequences of evil that reverberate on those who commit it, but those consequences often don't match the evil itself. If they did, then there would be no need of hell. Judgment would be ongoing, even now, which it's not.

In one sense, however, judgment has already occurred. God's

wrath and righteous indignation against sin and evil has been manifested. Hell, the second death, happened—but instead of happening right away to those who deserve it, it happened to Jesus Christ on the cross. What killed Christ was the wrath of a holy God who allowed Jesus to face divine wrath—the Lord's final righteous judgment against sin—so that none of us have to face the second death ourselves.

"But we see Jesus, who was made a little lower than the angels for the suffering of death, crowned with glory and honour; that he by the grace of God should taste death for every man" (Hebrews 2:9). That death He tasted was the second death, the one that the finally impenitent will have to meet as well because they didn't accept Christ's substitution.

"[T]he Lord has put on Him the iniquity of us all" (Isaiah 53:6). Just as all mankind went astray, Jesus took the sin of all mankind upon Himself in order that all mankind could be redeemed.

"Therefore as by the offence of one judgment came upon all men to condemnation; even so by the righteousness of one the free gift came upon all men unto justification of life" (Romans 5:18).

Christ was the "Lamb slain from the foundation of the world" (Revelation 13:8); it was planned, from the start, that Christ Himself—as our substitute—would face God's righteous wrath for sin so that, ideally, no one else would have to. The fires of hell were never meant for humans but were "prepared for the devil and his angels" (Matthew 25:41).

God originally intended that we all be saved—"Who will have all men to be saved, and to come unto the knowledge of the truth" (1 Timothy 2:4). We were predestined to be rescued from the destiny that fate handed us—"In whom also we have obtained an inheritance, being predestinated according to the purpose of him who worketh all things after the counsel of his own will" (Ephesians 1:11). All of us were ransomed by Jesus at the cross—"Who gave himself a ransom for all" (1 Timothy 2:6). If these things are true (and they are), then the punishment for the sins of *all the world* had to have fallen on Christ. "He is the propitiation for our sins: and not for ours only, but also for the sins of the whole world" (1 John 2:2, italics supplied).

This is what we believe—that Christ paid the penalty for the sins of everyone.

"Scripture teaches," said *Seventh-day Adventists Believe . . . A Biblical Exposition of 27 Fundamental Doctrines,* "the universal nature of Christ's substitutionary death. By 'the grace of God,' He experienced death for everyone (Hebrews 2:9). Like Adam, all have sinned (Romans 5:12), therefore, everyone experiences death—the first death. The death that Christ tasted for everyone was the second death—the full curse of death."[10]

What exactly does it mean to say that Christ tasted death for every man, that the sins of the whole world fell on Him? However much we have turned that concept into a Christian mantra, are we ready to accept its implications? Logic is easy, painless, except when taken to the bitter end.

It's the evening of May 31, 1962, a few hours before midnight, in Ramle prison, Israel. Adolph Eichmann, one of the coldest butchers in history, met with a Christian minister who presented the gospel to this genocidal monster and asked that he repent. Eichmann, we know, refused.

*But suppose he hadn't?* Suppose that this man, who diligently signed orders that sent millions—elderly, teenagers, infants, pregnant women, ten-year-olds—to horrible deaths, suppose he had truly repented? Suppose he had dropped to his knees and from the deepest depths of a heart shriveled with remorse confessed his evil and cried out for mercy and pardon from a merciful and pardoning God. Suppose crushed, broken, overwhelmed with remorse, he had fallen on his face and pled the righteousness of Jesus Christ as the only hope for his evil, twisted soul? Suppose he had acknowledged that he deserved only the worst damnation but, as a beggar holding out a broken cup, he sought mercy and grace instead. Suppose, not adhering to any merits of his own but only to Christ's, he claimed the promise of the Lord that "him that cometh to me I will in no wise cast out" (John 6:37) or that "whosoever shall call upon the name of the Lord shall be saved" (Romans 10:13) or "that whosoever believeth in him should not perish, but have everlasting life" (John 3:16)? Suppose Eichmann had beaten his breast, pleading for God to be merciful to him, admitting that all he could present to the Lord was filthy, sin-defiled garments. Suppose he sought with tears the garment of Christ's righteousness? Suppose he, under the unction of the Holy Spirit, had claimed the blood of Christ shed for the sins of the whole world?

Christ died for all men, right? "All men" includes Adolph Eichmann. This means that the punishment for Adolph Eichmann's sins—for that baby who chewed its fingers to nubs, for those 4,000 children sent on his orders to the gas chambers, for those little ones tossed alive into the flames, for that mother and baby machine-gunned in the ditch, for the millions of other deaths for which Eichmann was responsible—that punishment fell on Jesus, at the cross.

Christ, in His flesh, paid for the evil of Adolph Eichmann. God's wrath at what Eichmann had done (and how could a just God not be angry?) was poured out on Jesus long before Eichmann was even born, so that Eichmann, had he repented, could have been forgiven. Otherwise, why would Eichmann's sins have fallen on Christ if Eichmann couldn't have been saved? The fact that Christ died for Eichmann means that Eichmann could have had the eternal life that his crimes more than likely denied thousands, maybe millions, of others from ever receiving. Why would Christ die for someone who had no possibility of ever being saved?

It hardly seems fair that Eichmann—whatever human penalties he had to face for his butchery—could have been forgiven by God for that butchery, does it? It's not! Yet there is an inherent "unfair-ness" in the gospel itself, in the idea of the innocent dying for the guilty. In human terms, if one person commits a crime and another one is punished for it, an injustice has occurred. It's unfair that the innocent should pay for the crime of the guilty, especially if the guilty person goes free as a result of the innocent being punished.

Yet "unfairness" is the essence of the gospel. It's the premise on which salvation is based. Isaiah 53 is all about "unfairness;" vicarious atonement is nothing but the guilty going free while the innocent are punished—hardly the foundation of equity. The Cross embodies a paradox of the most extreme cases of both justice and injustice— justice because the demands of a violated law were met, and injustice because they were met in the body of one who had never violated the law. Anyone who is saved is not getting justice, for justice demands that the guilty be punished, and because we're all guilty we all should be punished. To be spared this punishment is to be spared what you deserve, and to be spared what you deserve is not to be treated fairly. As believers, we don't want fairness; we want mercy, grace, and pardon. Hell is God being fair.

There's a mystery, an essential tension, that seems to keep everything in place, as if the universe were glued together by paradoxes (or maybe these paradoxes don't exist except in our fallen minds?). The "unfairness" of the Cross, an "unfairness" that will spare untold numbers the punishment they deserve, is balanced with the scriptural promise, again and again, that God is just, and that justice will ultimately prevail. When this horrible experiment with sin is over, when the darkness and shadows that shroud our minds are replaced by the light of the Lord's unveiled countenance, when the evil that seems to hide for so many the goodness of God is finally and totally eradicated in the flames of hell—then we will rejoice in both the "unfairness" and the justice of God in ways that seem impossible now.

There, when the veil that darkens our vision shall be removed, and our eyes shall behold that world of beauty of which we now catch glimpses through the microscope; when we look on the glories of the heavens, now scanned afar through the telescope; when, the blight of sin removed, the whole earth shall appear in "the beauty of the Lord our God," what a field will be open to our study! There the student of science may read the records of creation and discern no reminders of the law of evil. . . . There will be open to the student, history of infinite scope and of wealth inexpressible. Not until he stands in the light of eternity will he see all things clearly. . . . Then will be opened before him the course of the great conflict that had its birth before time began, and that ends only when time shall cease. The history of the inception of sin; of fatal falsehood in its crooked working; of truth that, swerving not from its own straight lines, has met and conquered error—all will be made manifest. . . . For what was the great controversy permitted to continue throughout the ages? Why was it that Satan's existence was not cut short at the outset of his rebellion? *It was that the universe might be convinced of God's justice in His dealing with evil*[11] (italics supplied).

These are words I grasp, but by faith alone. Sight, at least what appears to my eyes now, doesn't hold such promise. Reality, stripped of any transcendence, of any hope of something beyond what nature alone provides, presents a bleak horizon. And history, if it's any precedent for the future, gives even less reason for optimism.

However much I believe in God, however clearly so much around me testifies to the existence of a Creator, however much I have known, personally, the love of God and have experienced, personally, His guiding providence and care—I can, at times, struggle with moments of doubt, and nothing so painfully sparks that twitch in my soul than the incessant evil that overloads my senses until they almost can't stand it anymore. Only by reaching out, not just beyond the narrow and parochial parameters of reason but beyond what I can see, feel, taste, touch, and hear—can I then, however sloppily, fit all the evil, Holocaust included, within my worldview. And that's only because my worldview is shaped by the revelation given to me by the Lord through His Word, a view of the world that takes me far beyond this world. And, included in this view, in fact a crucial part of it, is hell— where the justice for which this pathetic little planet pants will finally be revealed.

Some within the church shudder at the thought that God Himself would bring fire down from heaven and burn people; that act doesn't fit their human concept of love. They believe it demeans God, lowers Him to our level. Though they don't deny the reality of a hell fire, for them the second death is somehow the natural result of sin, as if something inherent in sin itself leads to its "reward" at the end of the millennium. Perhaps there's some truth to this position, and if that's what these folk need to get them through the day, fine (of course, they're probably saying the same thing about me and my view of hell, "If that's what he needs . . .").

Those drawn to that theology, however, in which the Lord is somewhat passive in the whole act of destroying the wicked in hell, usually tend to be white, Anglo-Saxon, middle or upper class Protestants who haven't known for themselves or their kin oppression, violence, persecution, and corporate injustice. Driving their fully-loaded cars, attending church in finely-decorated sanctuaries, brunching on their nice balconies that overlook nature in all its glory, with no wrenching historical consciousness to curdle their guts, with no brothers or sisters or family members bedecked in barbed wire, they can't possibly understand those of us whose marrow cries out for justice and divine retribution. Theirs is a "bourgeoisie theology," one that is lightly chattered about in summer homes and expensive watering holes, chatter not heard on factory floors or in the sweat of fields, nor which resonates in souls that bear the weight of unrequited evil—which is most of the world and much of the church. *We* have no problem with God Himself actively bringing just punishment upon the wicked. We'd have a problem if He didn't.

The Holocaust is my own personal hell; others have their own.

Yet whatever injustices, inequities, and blatant in-your-face-unpunished evil that mocks the very concept of morality and rightness and that turns your soul into a raging fire of anger—Isaiah, and much of the Bible, promises that our omnipotent, loving God will unfurl perfect justice at the end, whatever the metaphysics of the act. However utterly impossible it might seem to us now, however far removed this possibility is from even the reaches of human imagination, we have to believe that all the justice not done here will be done there; all the just punishment not received now will be received then.

But we have to wait, for we can't see it now. All we can do now is grasp it, by faith—for faith is the only medium by which the promise of justice can be seen, the only means by which it can become real to us. Nothing here portends, hints at, or alludes to it. What is here mocks it instead, which is why we need more than what our sense alone can give.

Thus, we have to anticipate hell, not with gleeful joy but with the solemn realization that God is just and that in His time and in His manner He will repay evil in a way that we never can. We have to reach out for that promise, that promise of hell.

And it is a promise. However angry I might feel over the Holocaust, or over all the evil that seems to defy even the very notion of an omnipotent God, much less a loving one—it's only the promise, the hope, that justice will be done that calms me, that neutralizes my bitterness, that helps me reconcile my knowledge and experience of a loving God in a world that is all but immunized to that love. The promise of hell helps answer the question of how a loving God can allow such evil. Evil must be, at least for now; but we have the promise, the promise of God Himself, that it will be answered for by those who commit it. Imagine if that promise didn't exist? What would it say about our world; and even more, what would it say about our God?

But God is just, and because God is just, because God promises to bring justice, we don't have to do so ourselves. For we could never

give evil the justice it deserves any more than the Israelis could give
Eichmann what he deserved by breaking his neck with a rope. The
promise of hell should lift the burden of vengeance off of those who
cry out for it now. Our justice, our vengeance, is too weak, too imper-
fect, too subjective to be real justice, real vengeance. But God knows
real justice, real vengeance, and His Word, His promise, is that in His
time we will see it. What we need to do now is believe it.

"Vengeance is mine; I will repay, saith the Lord" (Romans 12:19).

"Vengeance belongeth unto me, I will recompense, saith the Lord"
(Hebrews 10:30).

And, no doubt, and thank God, He will.

---

[1]Dylan Thomas, "The Hand That Signed the Paper," *Collected Poems* (New York: New
Directions, 1971), 71.

[2]Ethan Allen, *Reason, the Only Oracle of Man* (New York: Scholar's Fascimile & Reprints,
1940), 40 of index.

[3]Max Dimont, *Jews, God, and History* (New York:Signet Books, 1962), 383.

[4]Eva Fleischner, ed., *Auschwitz—Beginning of New Era? Reflections on the Holocaust*
(New York: Ktav Publishing House, 1977), 10.

[5]From Nechama Tec, *When Light Pierced Darkness: Christian Rescue of Jews in Nazi-
Occupied Poland* (New York: Oxford University Press, 1986), 111.

[6]From Nora Levin, *The Holocaust* (New York: Thomas Y. Crowell, 1968), 292.

[7]Kurt Cobain, "Lake of Fire," *Nirvana: Unplugged in New York*, Geffen Records.

[8]*Spiritual Gifts,* 1:118.

[9]Jacques Doukhan, *Daniel: The Vision of the End* (Berrien Springs, Mich.: Andrews University Press, 1989), 41.

[10]*Seventh-day Adventists Believe . . . A Biblical Exposition of 27 Fundamental Doctrines*
(Silver Spring, Md.: Ministerial Association of Seventh-day Adventists, 1988), 113, 114.

[11]*Education,* 301-308.

# Ultimate Things

*"All the treasures of the universe will be open to the study of God's redeemed. Unfettered by mortality, they wing their tireless flight to worlds afar—worlds that thrilled with sorrow at the spectacle of human woe and rang with songs of gladness at the tidings of a ransomed soul. With unutterable delight the children of earth enter into the joy and the wisdom of unfallen beings. . . . With undimmed vision they gaze upon the glory of creation—suns and stars and systems, all in their appointed order circling the throne of Deity. Upon all things, from the least to the greatest, the Creator's name is written, and in all are the riches of His power displayed. And the years of eternity, as they roll, will bring richer and still more glorious revelations of God and of Christ. As knowledge is progressive, so will love, reverence, and happiness increase. The more men learn of God, the greater will be their admiration of His character. As Jesus opens before them the riches of redemption and the amazing achievements in the great controversy with Satan, the hearts of the ransomed thrill with more fervent devotion, and with more rapturous joy they sweep the harps of gold; and ten thousand times ten thousand and thousands of thousands of voices unite to swell the mighty chorus of praise. The great controversy is ended. Sin and sinners are no more. The entire universe is clean. One pulse of harmony and gladness beats through the vast creation. From Him who created all, flow life and light and gladness, throughout the realms of illimitable*

*space. From the minutest atom to the greatest world, all things, animate and inanimate, in their unshadowed beauty and perfect joy declare that God is love." —Ellen G. White[1]*

In Greek mythology, Sisyphus had been condemned by the gods to push a rock to the top of a mountain, where it would of its own weight fall to the bottom. Sisyphus then had to shove it back up, only to have it roll down, again and again, the process continuing forever. The idea was that no punishment could be worse than futile, hopeless labor.

A few millennia after the story was first told, Frenchman Albert Camus titled a short book *The Myth of Sisyphus*. Written in 1940, during the Nazi occupation of France, the essay used Sisyphus as a metaphor of human existence itself. Because life has no meaning, Camus asked, is it worth living? If all the energy, effort, and passion needed to exist is like Sisyphus's labor, hopeless and futile—why bother?

"There is but one truly serious philosophical problem," Camus wrote, "and that is suicide. Judging whether life is or is not worth living amounts to answering the fundamental question of philosophy."[2]

Camus has a point, at least given his premise that there is no God, and thus this existence—with all its trials, pain, perplexities, and absurdities—is all that we have and are, and therefore is meaningless. According to Camus, our whole essence is contained in, and limited by, our own mortality. Nothing transcends it, nothing exceeds it. Our life is its own end, and because our end always dissolves into dust, what can it mean?

"Dying voluntarily implies that you have recognized, even instinctively, the ridiculous character of the habit, the absence of any profound reason for living, the insane character of that daily agitation, and the uselessness of suffering."[3]

A teenage boy, at seventeen, had been shot and killed. His brother, commenting on the kid's troubled past, cried out, "All for nothing!" But if human existence doesn't extend beyond the individual life itself, what's the qualitative difference between a teenager dead at seventeen and a sage dead at ninety-seven? It is still, in the end, "All for nothing!"

However depressing, Camus took his premises to their logical conclusion. If this pathetic little spasm of cellular metabolism defines all that we have or mean, then we don't have or mean much. And, considering that the little we possess is suffused with pain, despair, agony, rage, and helplessness, the whole human endeavor becomes absurd because it is meaningless. To live, suffer, and die for a purpose is hard enough; to go through it all for nothing is the essence of absurdity, especially when as humans we're able to envision something better.

Here is the real problem for Camus: Our awareness of what we are, as opposed to what we want to be, is a tension that chickens don't have. If we end up as the animals, we're no better off than they are. In fact, we're worse off because, unlike dogs and pigs, we can contemplate transcendence, eternity, and the chasm between what we are and what we desire to be. "Living," wrote Camus, "is keeping the absurd alive. Keeping it alive is contemplating it."[4] Humans contemplate it; oysters don't; that's why our existence (and not their's) is absurd.

Camus wasn't the only one to understand the utter futility of human existence if nothing followed it, if all we were or ever could be was consummated in the grave. Paul wrote:

> Now if Christ be preached that he rose from the dead, how say some among you that there is no resurrection of the dead? But if there be no resurrection of the dead, then is Christ not risen: And if Christ be not risen, then is our preaching vain, and your faith is also vain. Yea, and we are found false witnesses of God; because we have testified of God that he raised up Christ: whom he raised not up, if so be that the dead rise not. For if the dead rise not, then is not Christ raised: And if Christ be not raised, your faith is vain; ye are yet in your sins. Then they also which are fallen asleep in Christ are perished. If in this life only we have hope in Christ, we are of all men most miserable (1 Corinthians 15:12-19).

Whatever the specific theological issue, Paul's point is the same as Camus's (however different the frame of reference). If the dead aren't raised, if the grave is the final stop, if there's nothing beyond this life, then it's all miserable and insane. For Paul, if Christ weren't resurrected, then believers won't be either; and if we're not resurrected, then our faith—indeed our lives—are in vain. That's why the Bible, especially the New Testament, is so clear about the resurrection of the dead. Nothing we believe has any meaning without it.

And many of them who sleep in the dust of the earth will awake, some to everlasting life, some to reproach and everlasting contempt (Daniel 12:2).

Jesus answered and said unto them, Ye do err, not knowing the scriptures, nor the power of God. For in the resurrection they neither marry, nor are given in marriage, but are as the angels of God in heaven (Matthew 22:29, 30).

Marvel not at this: for the hour is coming, in which all that are in the graves shall hear his voice, and shall come forth; they that have done good, unto the resurrection of life; and they that have done evil, unto the resurrection of damnation (John 5:28, 29).

Jesus said unto her, I am the resurrection, and the life: he that believeth in me, though he were dead, yet shall he live (John 11:25).

But this I confess unto thee, that after the way which they call heresy, so worship I the God of my fathers, believing all things which are written in the law and in the prophets: And have hope toward God, which they themselves also allow, that there shall be a resurrection of the dead, both of the just and unjust (Acts 24:14, 15).

Then cometh the end, when he shall have delivered up the kingdom to God, even the Father; when he shall have put down all rule and all authority and power. For he must reign, till he hath put all enemies under his feet. The last enemy that shall be destroyed is death (1 Corinthians 15:24-26).

Behold, I shew you a mystery; We shall not all sleep, but we shall all be changed, in a moment, in the twinkling of an eye, at the last trump: for the trumpet shall sound, and the dead shall be raised incorruptible, and we shall be changed. For this corruptible must put on incorruption, and this mortal must put on immortality. So when this corruptible shall have put on incorruption, and this mortal shall have put on immortality, then shall be brought to pass the saying that is written, Death is swallowed up in victory. O death, where is thy sting? O grave, where is thy victory? (1 Corinthians 15:51-55).

But the rest of the dead lived not again until the thousand years were finished. This is the first resurrection. Blessed and holy is he that hath part in the first resurrection: on such the second death hath no power, but they shall be priests of God and of Christ, and shall reign with him a thousand years (Revelation 20:5, 6).

The resurrection of the dead isn't a hope—it is *the* hope. It is, for us, the final purpose of all that we believe. The Second Coming is where it all climaxes, where it is all consummated, where it all comes to fruition. At the resurrection of the dead our true purpose as human beings is realized. Anything prior to it, anything short of resurrection, leaves us incomplete, purposeless, without reason to be and even less reason to hope. Only at the Second Coming, only when the graves are opened, will life itself be vindicated and shown not to be the absurd and purposeless venture that it becomes if the graves stay closed. Without that promise, what is Christianity other than a dangling stone bone before the eyes of a starving, pawing dog? Without the Second Coming—where the dead in Christ will be resurrected to immortality while those who are alive will be given immortality too—the first coming is meaningless.

What is the purpose of the first coming if not the second? What good was Christ's death on the cross if it doesn't lead to the resurrection of the dead and to immortality? To be justified, to be redeemed, to be pardoned—what are these apart from the resurrection except bogus theological terms that no more reflect reality than *Star Trek* films reflect life in the old West. Without the Second Coming, Christ wasted His time at the first.

*But Christ left us a good example of how to live.* But so did Martin Luther King Jr., Mother Teresa, Mohatmas Ghandi, and Captain Kangaroo. We don't need just a good example. We need a Savior. More than we need someone who can tell us to turn the other cheek, to go the extra mile, or to love our enemies—we need someone who can raise our dried and crusted bones from the dirt, who can clothe our mortality with immortality, who can exchange our corruption for incorruption. Martin Luther King Jr., Mother Teresa, Mohatmas Ghandi, and Captain Kangaroo can't do that for us. Only Jesus can, and He will, at the Second Coming—which is why it, and it alone, is where all that we hope for becomes reality and the final and ultimate promises made by God become fulfilled in our flesh. It's only then that our faith in following Christ is fully vindicated.

We like to say that Christ completed His work at the cross. Nonsense. Nothing is completed, nothing, until all the redeemed are clothed with immortality in a world where sin will never rise again. Until then, everything is penultimate. Our hope lies only in the ultimate,[5] the Second Coming, without which nothing we believe makes sense.

What can grace, justification, salvation, or redemption mean without the return of Christ to clothe His saints with immortality? Nothing. That's why Scripture doesn't always separate the first and second coming. They're two parts of a whole. The first coming is the "ultimate," but only as consummated in the second. The two comings are so closely tied that it's not always easy in Scripture to tell them apart.

"Whereas the New Testament hope," wrote Niels-Erik Andreasen, "focuses exclusively upon the return of Christ, the Old Testament hope has two foci—the nearer first advent and the more distant second advent. Frequently both foci come to expression in a single picture."[6]

Such as in Isaiah. If Isaiah is "the gospel prophet," if his name itself means "Salvation is of the Lord," then his book by necessity would have to include the Second Coming, because the gospel and salvation are neutered terms apart from the Second Coming. There's no "good news," no salvation, without the Second Coming. For this reason Isaiah, so full of the first coming, is full of the Second Coming as well.

> And a rod shall come forth from the stem of Jesse, and a branch from his root will bear fruit. And the Spirit of the Lord will rest upon him, the Spirit of wisdom and understanding, the Spirit of counsel and might, the Spirit of knowledge and the fear of the Lord. And his delight will be in the fear of the Lord, and he will judge, but not in the sight of his eyes, nor in the hearing of his ears will he reprove. But he will judge the poor with righteousness, and he will reprove with uprightness the meek of the earth. Then with the breath of his mouth and with the Spirit of His lips He will slay the wicked. And righteousness will be the girdle of his waist and faithfulness of his loins. Then the wolf will dwell with the lamb, and the leopard with the kid will lie down; and the calf, the lion, and the fatling will be together, and a little child shall lead them (Isaiah 11:1-6).

Here, both comings are melded into this single prophetic utterance. The first few verses deal with Jesus' first advent; the rest are what happens at the second and after. They are tied together because they are parts of the whole; they are the two sides of a plane, the three sides of a triangle, the four sides of a square. The first and second comings must be understood as a unit. The first without the second is meaningless; the second without the first is impossible. However much time may separate them, they are one. How can the following verses be understood, apart from both comings being depicted in one picture?

> For a son is born to us, to us a child is given, and dominion will be on his shoulder, and they will call his name Wonderful Counselor, Mighty God, Everlasting Father, Prince of Peace. And there will be no end to the growth of his dominion and to our peace. To establish it [dominion] upon the throne of David and upon his kingdom, and to support it with justice and righteousness, from now and for ever (Isaiah 9:6, 7).

All through the "gospel prophet" the Second Coming—and beyond—is revealed, in one facet or another, with literal and figurative language, because the gospel can find its meaning in the Second Coming alone, for only then the righteous are resurrected to eternal life.

> He will swallow up death forever, and the Lord God will wipe away tears from all faces; then the reproaches of his people he will take away from all the earth, for the Lord has spoken. And it will be said in that day, "Behold, this is our God, we have waited for him, and he will save us. This is our God, we have waited for him. Let us rejoice and be glad in his salvation" (Isaiah 25:8, 9).

> Your dead will live. My body will rise. Awake and sing you who dwell in the dust, for your dew is as the dew of the dawn, and the earth will cast out the dead (Isaiah 26:19).
> Lift up your eyes toward heaven and look to the earth beneath, for heaven as smoke will vanish, and the earth as a garment will wear out, and its inhabitants in a like manner will die. But my salvation will be forever and my righteousness will not be abolished. For the moth will eat them like a garment, and the worm will eat

them like wool, but righteousness will be forever and my salvation from generation to generation (Isaiah 51:6, 8).

> For, behold, I create a new heaven and a new earth; the former will not be remembered or come to mind. But be glad, and rejoice for ever, in what I create. For, behold, I create Jerusalem a joy, and her people for gladness. . . . And they will build houses, and they will dwell in them, and they will plant vineyards and eat the fruit. They will not build, and another dwell there; they will not plant and another eat. . . . The wolf and the lamb shall feed as one, and the lion like the ox will eat straw, and dust shall be the serpent's food (Isaiah 65:17, 21, 22, 25).

Here's how Ellen White uses Isaiah to describe what it will be like after Christ returns:

> As the prophet beholds the redeemed dwelling in the City of God, free from sin and from all marks of the curse, in rapture he exclaims, "Rejoice ye with Jerusalem, and be glad with her, all ye that love her: rejoice for joy with her.
>
> "Violence shall no more be heard in thy land,
> Wasting nor destruction within thy borders;
> But thou shalt call thy walls Salvation,
> And thy gates Praise.
>
> "The sun shall be no more thy light by day;
> Neither for brightness shall the moon give light unto thee:
> But the Lord shall be unto thee an everlasting light,
> And thy God thy glory.
>
> "Thy sun shall no more go down;
> Neither shall thy moon withdraw itself:

For the Lord shall be thine everlasting light,
And the days of thy mourning shall be ended.

"Thy people also shall be all righteous:
They shall inherit the land forever,
The branch of My planting,
The work of My hands,
That I may be glorified."
—Isaiah 66:10; 60:18, 21.[7]

For as the new heavens and the new earth, which I make,
stand before me, says the Lord, thus your seed and your name
will stand. And it will come to pass, from one new moon to
another, and from one Sabbath to another, will come all flesh to
worship before me, says the Lord (Isaiah 66:22, 23).

At the Second Coming, all that is earthly and man-made, and
thus temporal and meaningless, is swept away under the power of
God, which will be revealed with a might and majesty never before
seen in the human realm. If the Cross accomplished what is beyond
the power of humans to do for themselves, how much more so the
Second Coming? At Christ's return, in mocking defiance of all human logic, reason, and science, in an act that exposes the world's
wisdom in all it parochialness, prejudices, and limits, the Lord will
appear in heaven and with the same voice that spoke light and life
into existence, He will speak again. Then, through the power of His
Word, the dead—whether in soft-pillowed caskets or in the bellies of
fish and squid or whether nothing but molecules in the stem of a
plant—will rise and be reconstructed in bodies far surpassing anything mankind ever possessed with the exception of Adam and Eve
before the Fall. That is God's ultimate promise—and it's the one promise that gives all the others any meaning at all.

In 1994, well-known physicist Frank J. Tipler wrote a book titled *The*

*Physics of Immortality.* He begins with these words: "This book is a description of the Omega Point Theory, which is a testable theory for an omnipresent, omniscient, omnipotent God who will one day in the far future resurrect every single one of us to live forever in an abode which is in all essentials the Judeo-Christian heaven. Every single term in the theory—for example 'omnipresent,' 'omniscient,' 'omnipotent,' 'resurrection (spiritual) body,' 'Heaven'—will be introduced as pure physical concepts. In this book I shall make no appeal, anywhere, to revelation. I shall appeal instead to the solid results of modern physical science; the only appeal will be the reader's reason. I shall describe the physical mechanism of the universal resurrection. I will show exactly why this power to resurrect, which modern physics allows, will actually exist in the far future, and why it will in fact be used. If any reader has lost a loved one, or is afraid of death, modern physics says: 'Be comforted, you and they shall live again.' "[8]

Whether Tipler actually proves what he says he does is more than doubtful, and the book does get more bizarre, if not almost philosophically incoherent, with each page. Yet, even if he has the means wrong, Tipler has the event right, and that's the resurrection of the dead.

Fortunately, we have better reasons to believe in the resurrection than Frank Tipler's dubious Omega Point Theory. And one reason is found in Daniel 2—the sheer odds alone, presented so forcefully and irrefutably in the chapter, give powerful evidence for us to trust in the promise of Jesus' coming and the eternity that it ushers in. The famous statute of gold, silver, bronze, iron, and clay in Nebuchadnezzar's dream isn't really about history; it's about a God who will redeem lost souls by giving them eternal life in a whole new existence.

In chapter 2, Daniel explains that the metals of the statute symbolize world empires that would rise and fall. History shows that Babylon, "the head of gold" (verse 38) did, indeed, come and go just as Daniel had predicted. The second kingdom, Media Persia, ("and in your place another kingdom will arise, earthier than you" [verse

39]) also came and went, as predicted. The third kingdom, Greece, ("and a third kingdom, another, of brass which will rule over all the earth" [verse 39]) came and went—again, as predicted. The fourth kingdom, pagan Rome, ("and the fourth kingdom will be strong as iron" [verse 40]) rose and fell—again according to the prophecy. Next, Daniel said that this fourth kingdom—unlike the others, which were each replaced by another single empire—would instead be broken up into lesser kingdoms, some stronger than others, and that these kingdoms would never be united, even through the bonds of family and marriage. "And that you saw the feet and the toes, partly clay, partly iron, the kingdom shall be divided . . . and as the toes of the feet were partly iron and partly clay, the kingdom will be partly strong and partly broken. And as you saw the iron mixed with the clay, they shall mingle themselves with men's seed, but they will not cleave one to another, even as iron will not mix with clay" (Daniel 2:41-43). What better—and more accurate—prediction could have been made about the breakup of the pagan Roman empire into what ultimately has become the divided nations (some weak, some strong) of modern, intermarried Europe?

What's left? Only God establishing His eternal kingdom, which is what happens after the Second Coming and the dead are raised to eternal life. "And in the days of those kings will the God of heaven set up an everlasting kingdom that will not be destroyed" (verse 44).

Look at the odds. Babylon, Media-Persia, Greece, pagan Rome, modern Europe—all came in order, just as Daniel had predicted (notice, too, that the Lord has here given us something as concrete, irrefutable, and as accessible as world history upon which to help establish our faith). The only kingdom left in the prophecy, and the only one that we, from our perspective, haven't yet seen fulfilled, is the last, Christ's eternal kingdom, which is established after the dead are resurrected.

What the Lord presents in this chapter are odds, five out of six, that the promise of His coming, the resurrection of the dead, and the establishment of His kingdom will be fulfilled. Daniel was right on the first five. Who could not trust him on the sixth?

Yet even five-out-of-six odds, however good, aren't good enough. God has given us something better, something by which we can know for sure the reality of His promise—and that is the Cross. If the first coming means nothing apart from the second, and the second means nothing apart from the resurrection of the dead (after all, what good is Christ's Second Coming if the dead are not raised?)—then the Cross is our guarantee that we will rise again.

At Calvary, Christ paid a ransom for our souls; why would He not retrieve what cost Him so dearly? We all believe that Christ, with His body, with His flesh, redeemed us from death. But what can that mean apart from the resurrection? Why would He suffer the wrath of God against sin if He doesn't resurrect sinners to eternal life? How could He promise that through His being lifted up He would draw all men unto Himself if men stay in the grave? The surety of His return is sealed in His blood. As certain as we are that Christ died on the cross for our sins, we can be just as sure that we will rise from the grave.

In Fyodor Dostoyevsky's greatest novel, *The Brothers Karamazov*, Ivan Karamazov says to his brother Aloysha, a monk: "Let me make it plain. I believe like a child that suffering will be healed and made up for, that all the humiliating absurdity of human contradictions will vanish like a pitiful mirage, like the despicable fabrication of the impotent and infinitely small Euclidian mind of man, that in the world's finale, at the moment of eternal harmony, something so precious will come to pass that it will suffice all hearts, for the comforting of all resentments, for the atonement of all the crimes of humanity, of all the blood they've shed; that it will make it not only be possible to forgive but to justify all that has happened with men—but though all that may come to pass, I don't accept it, I won't accept it."[9]

But we *must* accept it; otherwise, we have only the "humiliating absurdity of human contradictions" to show for all the major and

petty grievances and pains we've inflicted on others and have ourselves received. We *must* accept it, because without it we might as
well seek immortality among the stars on the tail of Hale-Bopp as
did those poor souls at Rancho Sante Fe. We *must* accept it; if not,
we'll have no hope of ever seeing our loved ones again, no hope of
having the unanswerable questions answered, no hope of ever seeing
the face of God or knowing the fullness of His love.

The Second Coming, the resurrection of the dead, isn't epilogue,
isn't appendix, isn't afterword; it's the *raison d'etre* of all the pages,
all the scenes, all the dialogues and transitions and chapters and sentences and commas and periods that precede it. We must, then, reach
out and stretch every nerve, every fiber, every synapse, and grasp by
faith this promise of something that we can't now see, feel, intuit, or
rationalize.

In fact, all we can do is read about it. Why? Because the wind in
the trees doesn't tell us about salvation; the stars at night don't herald
in letters of fire the promise of eternal life; the waves don't roar promises of the first resurrection in our ears; the birds chirping outside
our bedroom windows don't express it (and, in fact, without the resurrection, the birds are really singing our dirges). We know about the
promise of His coming and the resurrection to life only because the
Word of God (and the Spirit of Prophecy) tell us about it. Without
them, how could we possibly know the only hope we have?

Thus, we must relentlessly eradicate from our list of possibilities
all that casts subtle doubts and flickering shadows on the authority of
the Bible (and the Spirit of Prophecy, for when one goes the other
soon follows). These alone give us the promise of the Second Coming and the resurrection. Nothing else—nothing in nature, logic, reason, science (Omega Point Principle included)—testifies so clearly
to it. Logic, reason, science, in and of themselves, tell us that when
we die we turn into nothing but carbon and dust, and that the closest
we'll come to life again is when we fertilize a tree or feed the bacteria
that dissolve us.

How logical is it, then, to allow these things (science, logic, reason) to weaken our trust in the Bible? Given what we do know, it would be illogical and unreasonable to let logic and reason cause us to question the authority that reveals to us the only hope we have—a hope that at its essence defies logic and reason and the painful limitations that they have placed on the human mind.

But Isaiah, "the gospel prophet," pours out upon us pages of reasons to trust in the "unreasonable." Through Isaiah's quill the Lord cries out, "Come, and let us reason together" (Isaiah 1:18). God has provided so many *reasons* to hope, to trust, to look beyond what we can see or rationalize or understand, and to grasp the promise that through Christ we can and will have an existence too wonderful for anything we can even dare imagine. Whatever the pains, whatever the discouragements, whatever the fears that stalk those living on a planet polluted in sin and poisoned in lies, Isaiah is an eloquent testimony that what we see here, that what life ignominiously dumps on us now, is *not* what we will ultimately get. What we've suffered here and now, in contrast to what we will rejoice in then and there, can't be compared, because what we get then and there will more than make up for what we've gotten here and now.

No matter how tired, how discouraged, how sorrowful and sore we are, Isaiah pleads, "Don't give up. Don't stop hoping. Don't stop trusting. Don't stop believing. Don't stop waiting." Because the moment we do we're in danger of making it all count for nothing when according to God's purposes it's all for something, something in the end so wonderful and perfect and happy and harmonious that we can only begin to dare to envision. We can't go by moods, by feelings, by the flow of hormones or neurotransmitters but only by the raw, naked promises of a God who cannot lie and who has promised us—a promise sealed in the blood of Jesus—that we will live again in a world without a single element of what makes this one so painful. Through Isaiah, God is stretching us beyond the confines of what we can see, hear, smell, taste, or reason with the dying sinful mass of matter that hums within our head; He is pointing us to something far beyond what the mere "Euclidian mind of man" on its own can foresee and understand, much less believe. Isaiah tells us what we can never learn or know for ourselves—that this bleeding, dying planet with its bleeding, dying beings isn't really our home. Instead, eternity with Jesus, where every pain is atoned for, where every tear is finally and forever wiped dry, where it's all done right—this is our home, this is where it all comes to, this is what Christ died on the cross to give us. It is *the* promise, the only one that truly matters, the promise without which nothing we believe or experience can have any meaning, the promise by which all things become righteous, holy, and true because all things unrighteous, unholy, and untrue will no longer be.

---

[1]*The Great Controversy,* 677, 678.

[2]Albert Camus, *The Myth of Sisyphus,* translated by Justin O'Brien (New York: Vintage Books, 1955), 3.

[3]*Ibid.,* 5.

[4]*Ibid.,* 40.

[5]"Justification by grace and faith alone," wrote Bonhoeffer, "remains in every respect the final word and for this reason, when we speak of the things before the last, we must not speak of them as having any value of their own, but we must bring to light their relation to the ultimate. It is for the sake of the ultimate that we must now speak of the penultimate." Dietrich Bonhoeffer, *Ethics* (New York: Collier Books, 1986), 125.

For Bonhoeffer, justification by faith, the "coming of grace," is the last thing, the ultimate, but it can be so only because it's all part of the Second Coming.

[6]Neils-Erik Andreasen, "The Advent Hope in the Old Testament," in *The Advent Hope in Scripture and History,* V. Norskov Olsen, ed. (Hagerstown, Md.: Review and Herald, 1987), 15.

[7]*Prophets and Kings,* 729.

[8]Frank. J. Tipler, *The Physics of Immortality* (New York: Doubleday & Co., 1994), 1.

[9]Fyodor Dostoyevsky, *The Brothers Karamazov* (New York:Oxford University Press, 1985), 264, 265.